C000093451

WITH
Elisabeth Smith

FAST RUSSIAN

HODDER
EDUCATION
AN HACHETTE UK COMPANY

The author would like to thank Rachel Farmer and Alexandra Borodulina, who acted as language consultants in the preparation of this book.

For UK order enquiries: please contact Bookpoint Ltd, 130 Milton Park, Abingdon, Oxon OX14 4SB. *Telephone*: +44 (0) 1235 827720. Fax: +44 (0) 1235 400454. Lines are open 09.00–17.00, Monday to Saturday, with a 24-hour message answering service. Details about our titles and how to order are available at www.teachyourself.com

For USA order enquiries: please contact McGraw-Hill Customer Services, PO Box 545, Blacklick, OH 43004-0545, USA. *Telephone*: 1-800-722-4726. Fax: 1-614-755-5645.

For Canada order enquiries: please contact McGraw-Hill Ryerson Ltd, 300 Water St, Whitby, Ontario L1N 9B6, Canada. *Telephone*: 905 430 5000. Fax: 905 430 5020.

Long renowned as the authoritative source for self-guided learning – with more than 50 million copies sold worldwide – the teach yourself series includes over 500 titles in the fields of languages, crafts, hobbies, business, computing and education.

British Library Cataloguing in Publication Data: a catalogue record for this title is available from the British Library.

Library of Congress Catalog Card Number: on file.

First published in UK 2000 as *Teach Yourself Instant Russian* by Hodder Education, part of Hachette UK, 338 Euston Road, London NW1 3BH.

First published in US 2000 as *Teach Yourself Instant Russian* by The McGraw-Hill Companies, Inc.

This edition published 2011.

The teach yourself name is a registered trade mark of Hodder Headline.

Typeset by MPS Limited, a Macmillan Company.

Printed in Great Britain for Hodder Education, an Hachette UK Company, 338 Euston Road, London NW1 3BH, by CPI Cox & Wyman, Reading, Berkshire RG1 8EX.

The publisher has used its best endeavours to ensure that the URLs for external websites referred to in this book are correct and active at the time of going to press. However, the publisher and the author have no responsibility for the websites and can make no guarantee that a site will remain live or that the content will remain relevant, decent or appropriate.

Hachette UK's policy is to use papers that are natural, renewable and recyclable products and made from wood grown in sustainable forests. The logging and manufacturing processes are expected to conform to the environmental regulations of the country of origin.

Impression number   10 9 8 7 6 5 4 3 2 1
Year   2014 2013 2012 2011

Contents

Read this first

If, like me, you usually skip introductions, don't! Read on! You need to know how **Fast Russian with Elisabeth Smith** works and why. You'll want to know how you are going to speak Russian in just six weeks.

When I decided to write this series I first called it *Barebones*, because that's what you want: no frills, no fuss, just the bare bones and go! So in **Fast Russian with Elisabeth Smith** you'll find:

- Only 461 words to say, well ... nearly everything.
- No tricky grammar – just some useful tips.
- No time wasters such as *the pen of my aunt...*
- No phrase book phrases for vodka sampling sessions in Siberia.
- No need to be perfect. Mistakes won't spoil your success.

I've put some 30 years of teaching experience into this course. I know how people learn. I also know how long they are motivated by a new project before the boredom sets in (a few weeks). And I am well aware how little time they can spare to study each day (just over ½ hour). That's why you'll complete **Fast Russian with Elisabeth Smith** in six weeks and get away with 45 minutes a day.

Of course there is some learning to do, but I have tried to make it as much fun as possible. You'll meet Tom and Kate Walker on holiday in Russia. They do the kind of things you need to know about: shopping, eating out and getting about. They chat to the locals, ask a lot of questions and even understand the answers – most of the time! As you will note, Tom and Kate speak Russian all the time, even to each other. What paragons of virtue!

To get the most out of this course, there are only three things you really should do:

- Follow the **Day-by-day** guide as suggested. Please don't skip bits and short-change your success. Everything is there for a reason.

- If you are a complete beginner and have only bought the book, treat yourself to the recording as well. It will help you to speak faster and with confidence.
- Don't skip the next page (**How this book works**). It's essential for your success.

When you have filled in your **Certificate** at the end of the book and can speak **Fast Russian with Elisabeth Smith**, I would like to hear from you. Why not visit my website www.elisabeth-smith.co.uk, e-mail me at elisabeth.smith@hodder.co.uk, or write to me care of Hodder Education, 338 Euston Road, London, NW1 3BH?

And please join me on:

Facebook at www.facebook.com/elisabethsmithlanguages

Twitter at www.twitter.com/LanguagesESmith

How this book works

Fast Russian with Elisabeth Smith has been structured for your rapid success. This is how it works:

Day-by-day guide Stick to it. If you miss a day, add one.

Dialogues Follow Tom and Kate through Russia. The English is in 'Russian-speak' to get you tuned in. 'Russian-speak' is English imitating the expressions and word order of Russian: We have a house big without telephone. You'll soon get a feel for the language.

New words Don't fight them, don't skip them – learn them! The **Flash cards** and the recording will help you. Get your friends or family to test you. Or take the **Flash cards** with you when you are out and about.

Good news grammar After you read it you can forget half and still succeed! That's why it's good news.

Flash words and flash sentences Read about these building blocks in the **Flash card** section. Then use them! They'll reduce learning time by 50%.

Learn by heart Obligatory! Memorizing puts you on the fast track to speaking in full sentences. When you know all six pieces you'll be able to speak in Russian for six minutes without drawing breath.

Let's speak Russian You will be doing the talking – in Russian.

Let's speak more Russian – fast and fluently Optional extras for more speaking practice without pausing and stumbling.

Spot the keys Listen to rapid Russian and make sense of it. Find the key words among a seemingly unintelligible string of sentences and get the gist of what's being said – an essential skill.

Say it simply Learn how to use simple Russian to say what you want to say. Don't be shy.

Test your progress Mark your own test and be amazed by the result.

Answers This is where you'll find the answers to the exercises.

◀ This icon asks you to switch on the recording.

Pronunciation If you don't know about it and don't have the recording go straight to **Week 1 Pronunciation**. You need to know about pronunciation before you can start Week 1.

Progress chart Enter your score each week and monitor your progress. Are you going for very good or outstanding?

Dictionary Forgotten one of the new words? Look it up in the dictionary.

Certificate It's on the last page. In six weeks it will have your name on it.

Progress chart

At the end of each week record your test score on the progress chart below.

At the end of the course throw out your worst result – anybody can have a bad week – and add up your five best weekly scores. Divide the total by five to get your average score and overall course result. Write your result – *outstanding*, *excellent*, *very good* or *good* – on your **Certificate** at the end of the book.

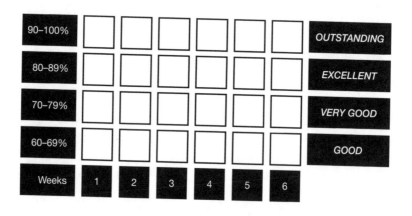

Total of five best weeks =

divided by five =

Your final result _____ %

Week 1

Day-by-day guide

Study for 45 minutes a day – or a little longer if you can!

Day zero
- Open the book and read **Read this first**.
- Now read **How this book works**.

Day one
- Read **In the aeroplane**.
- Listen to/Read **F samalyotee**.
- Listen to/Read the **New words**, then learn some of them.

Day two
- Repeat **F samalyotee** and the **New words**.
- Listen to/Read **Pronunciation**.
- Learn more **New words**.

Day three
- Learn all the **New words** until you know them well.
- Use the **Flash words** to help you.
- Read and learn the **Good news grammar**.

Day four
- Cut out and learn the **Flash sentences**.
- Listen to/Read **Learn by heart.**

Day five
- Listen to/Read **Let's speak Russian.**
- Revise! Tomorrow you'll be testing your progress.

Day six
- Listen to/Read **Let's speak more Russian** (optional).
- Listen to/Read **Let's speak Russian – fast and fluently** (optional).
- Translate **Test your progress**.

Day seven – This is your day off!

In the aeroplane

Tom and Kate Walker are on their way to Russia. They board a plane to Yalta via Moscow and squeeze past Yuriy Zhivago who is sitting in their row.

Don't forget that the English is in 'Russian-speak' to help you get used to the way the language works.

Tom   Excuse me, please, by us (we have) seats 9a and 9b.

Yuriy   Yes?... little minute (just a moment), please.

Tom   Hello. We – Tom and Kate Walker.

Yuriy   Hello. Me they call (I am called) Zhivago.

Tom   Dr Zhivago?

Yuriy   No, unfortunately. I – Yuriy Zhivago.

Tom   We are going to Yalta. You also?

Yuriy   No, I am going to Moscow. But I from Novgorod.

Tom   Novgorod very beautiful town. I was there in May, on business.

Yuriy   Who you? (What do you do?)

Tom   I programmer. Computers. I work at Unilever.

Yuriy   And you, Mrs Walker? Who you? Where do you work?

Kate   I worked in travel agency. Now I work in Rover. The work there better.

Yuriy   You from London?

Kate   No, we from Manchester. We were three years in London and a year in New York. Now we in Birmingham.

Yuriy   I worked in the university. Now I work in bank.

Kate   Work in bank good?

Yuriy   Work boring. But money (of money) more. By me (I have) big flat, Mercedes, wife, son and daughter. My wife from America. By her (she has) parents in Los Angeles and girlfriend in Florida. She always rings to them. It (is) costs expensive.

F samalyotee

🔊 CD1, tr 2

Tom and Kate Walker are on their way to Russia. They board a plane to Yalta via Moscow and squeeze past Yuriy Zhivago who is sitting in their row.

The letters in bold indicate the stress the syllable in which they appear. The first word of the dialogue below is *excuse me* – 'eez-vee-**nee**-tee'. You would stress the penultimate syllable. When you find a bold o you pronounce it like the o in *bore*. If it isn't bold it's like the a in *sofa*.

Tom   Eezveen**ee**tee, pazh**a**loosta, oo nas meest**a** 9a ee 9b.

Yuriy   Da?... meen**oo**tachkoo, pazh**a**loosta.

Tom   Zdr**a**stvooiytee. Mi – Tom ee Kate Walker.

Yuriy   Zdr**a**stvooiytee. Meen**ya** zav**oo**t Zhiv**a**ga.

Tom   D**o**ktar Zhiv**a**ga?

Yuriy   Nyet, k sazhil**ye**neeyu. Ya –**Yu**riy Zhiv**a**ga.

Tom   Mi **ye**deem v **Ya**ltoo. Vi t**o**zhe?

Yuriy   Nyet. Ya **ye**doo v Maskv**oo**. No ya eez N**o**vgarada.

Tom   N**o**vgarat **o**cheen' kras**ee**viiy g**o**rat. Ya tam bil v m**a**ee, pa b**ee**znisoo.

Yuriy   Kto vi?

Tom   Ya pragram**ee**st. Kamp'**yu**tiri. Ya rab**o**tayu v Oonee**lee**veeerye.

Yuriy   A vi, m**ee**sees Walker? Kto vi? Gdee vi rab**o**taeetee?

Kate   Ya rab**o**tala v toorag**ye**ntstvee. Seech**ya**s ya rab**o**tayu v R**o**veerye. Rab**o**ta tam l**oo**chshe.

Yuriy   Vi eez L**o**ndana?

Kate   Nyet. Mi eez Manch**ye**s'teera. Mi b**i**lee tree g**o**da v L**o**ndanee ee got v Nyu Y**o**rkee. Seech**ya**s mi v Beermeeng**ye**mee.

Yuriy   Ya rab**o**tal v ooneeveerseet**ye**tee. Seech**ya**s ya rab**o**tayu v b**a**nkee.

Kate   Rab**o**ta v b**a**nkee khar**o**shaya?

Yuriy   Rab**o**ta sk**oo**chnaya. No d**ye**neek b**o**l'shi. Oo meen**ya** bal'sh**a**ya kvart**ee**ra, Meers**ee**d**e**s, zhin**a**, sin ee doch. M**a**ya zhin**a** eez Am**ye**reekee. Oo nee**yo** rad**ee**teeli v Los **A**nzhileesee ee padr**oo**ga v Flar**ee**dee. An**a** vs**ee**gd**a** zvan**ee**t eem. **E**ta st**o**eet d**o**raga.

3

| **Kate** | We now in holiday (on holiday). You also? |
| **Yuriy** | No, unfortunately. By me (I have) in August holiday. We are going to Greece. By us (we have) there house… summer home – without telephone. And we go there without mobile phone! |

New words

🔊 CD1, tr 3

Learning words the traditional way can be boring. If you enjoy the **Flash cards** why not make your own for the rest of the words? Always say the words out loud.

v, va, f *in, to, at*
samal**yo**t(ee) *aeroplane*
eezveen**ee**tee *excuse me*
pazh**a**loosta *please*
oo nas *by us (we have)*
meest**a** *places, seats*
a… b a… b *(pronounced ah… bay)*
ee *and*
da *yes*
meen**oo**tachkoo *little minute*
zdr**a**stvooiytee *hello*
mi *we*
meen**ya** zav**oo**t *they call me (I am called)*
nyet *no*
k sazhil**ye**neeyu *unfortunately*
ya *I*
yedeem *we go (travel)*
yedoo *I go (travel)*
vi *you (polite)*
t**o**zhe *also*
no *but*
eez, ees *from*
ocheen' *very*
kras**ee**viiy *beautiful*
g**o**rad, g**o**rat *town*
tam *there*
bil *was*
bilee *were*

v m**a**ee *in May*
dlya *for*
pa b**ee**znisoo *on business*
kto *who*
rab**o**tayu *I work*
rab**o**taeetee *you work*
pragram**ee**st *computer programmer*
kamp'**yu**tir/kamp'**yu**tiri *computer*
gdye *where*
rab**o**tala *I, she worked*
rab**o**tal *I, he worked*
v toorag**ye**ntstvee *in a/the travel agency*
seech**ya**s *now*
rab**o**ta *work, job*
l**oo**chshe *better*
tree *three*
g**o**da/g**o**t *year*
v ooneeveerseet**ye**tee *at a/the university*
bank/v b**a**nkee *bank/in, at bank*
khar**o**chaya *good*
sk**oo**chnaya *boring*
d**ye**neek *money*
b**o**l'shi *more*
oo meen**ya** *I have*
bal'sh**a**ya *big*
kvart**ee**ra *flat*

4

Kate Mi seechyas v otpooskee. Vi tozhe?

Yuriy Nyet, k sazhilyeneeyu. Oo meenya v avgoostee otpoosk.
Mi **ye**deem v Gryetsiyu. Oo nas tam dom… dachya – bees
teeleefona. Mi **ye**deem tooda bees sotavava!

maya, moiy *my*		eta *it is*	
zhina *wife*		stoeet *costs*	
sin *son*		doraga *expensive*	
doch *daughter*		v otpooskee *on holiday*	
oo neeyo *she has*		v avgoos'tee *in August*	
radeeteelee *parents*		tam *there*	
padrooga *girlfriend*		dom *house*	
ana *she*		dachya *summer house*	
vseegda *always*		bees teeleefona *without telephone*	
zvaneet *rings, phones*		sotaviy (teeleefon) *mobile*	
eem *to them*		telephone	

> TOTAL NEW WORDS: 75…
> only 306 words to go!

Some easy extras
Myeseetsi *(months)*

yanvar', feevral', mart, apryel', maiy, eeyun', eeyul', avgoost,
seentyabr', aktyabr', nayabr', deekabr'

Tsifri *(numerals)*

adeen	1	shes't'	6
dva	2	syem'	7
tree	3	voseem'	8
cheetiree	4	dyeveet'	9
pyat'	5	dyeseet'	10

More greetings
dobraye ootra *good morning* dobriiy dyen' *good day, good
afternoon* dobriiy vyecheer *good evening* da sveedaneeya *goodbye*

5

Pronunciation

◀)) CD1, tr 4

The Russian language is beautiful, so drop all inhibitions and try to speak Russian rather than English with the words changed.

As you can see, all the words in **Fast Russian with Elisabeth Smith** have been transliterated into phonetic language. That makes it much easier, especially if you are in a hurry. You don't have to learn the Cyrillic alphabet first but can start speaking straight away.

The guide to vowels and consonants will get you started. Sometimes it takes a lot of English letters – for example **shsh** – to produce the sound of one Russian letter, but you'll soon pick it up.

And don't worry if you don't get it exactly right. Near enough is good enough.

Vowels

Say the sound out loud and then the Russian example out loud.

a	like *a* in *father*	bal'sh**a**ya
e	like *e* in *let*	**e**ta
ee	like *ee* in *feet*	eezveen**ee**tee
i	like *i* in *still*	m**i**
iy	like *y* in *boy*	kras**ee**viiy
o	like *o* in *bore*	L**o**ndan
oo	like *oo* in *shoot*	l**oo**chshee

y plus vowel

ya	like *ya* in *yard*	ya
ye	like *ye* in *yet*	nyet
yo	like *yo* in *yonder*	oo nee**yo**
yu	like *u* in *universal*	ya rab**o**tayu

Consonants

g	is always pronounced as a 'hard' *g*, as in *goat*	
r	is rolled (as in Italian)	
v	like *v* in *vase*	
zh	like *s* in *pleasure*	t**o**zhe
kh	like *ch* in *loch*	khar**o**shaya
ts	like *ts* in *quits*	tsar
sh	like *sh* in *shout*	shes't'
shsh	like *sh* in *posh ship*	eeshsh**yo**
l', t'		sk**o**l'ka
iy	like *y* in *toy*	m**a**iy

When you see a ' after a letter try to slip in a very soft *y*.

Accent

The letter in **bold** tells you to stress the syllable in which it appears. Example: Maskv**oo**, rab**o**tayu. The stress is especially important when you come across the vowel **o**. If it is stressed, it is pronounced like the *o* in *bore*; if it is not stressed, it is pronounced like the *a* in *sofa*.

When you go to Russia you'll want to know a little of the Cyrillic script, too. So, as an introduction, here's the Russian alphabet. And later in the course there'll also be a few useful flash words in 'real' Russian script, to help you on your way.

А	Б	В	Г	Д	Е	Ё	Ж	З	И	Й	К	Л	М	Н	О	П	Р
а	б	в	г	д	е	ё	ж	з	и	й	к	л	м	н	о	п	р
С	Т	У	Ф	Х	Ц	Ч	Ш	Щ	Ъ	Ы	Ь	Э	Ю	Я			
с	т	у	ф	х	ц	ч	ш	щ	ъ	ы	ь	э	ю	я			

Good news grammar

🔊 CD1, tr 5

This is the good news part of each week. Remember I promised *no ghastly grammar*! I simply explain the differences between Russian and English. This will help you to speak Russian.

1 Words for 'the' and 'a'

There aren't any! So bank in Russian means either *a bank* or *the bank* and the plural bankee means either *some banks* or *the banks*.

2 The Russian words for 'am', 'are', 'is'

There aren't any! So all you need to say in Russian is:

I computer programmer = ya pragram**ee**st

3 The Russian words for 'have', 'has'

There aren't any! Russian uses a different sort of phrase and says, literally, *by me (there is)* = Oo meen**ya**.

Example: I have a flat. = Oo meen**ya** kvart**ee**ra.

Here is the complete list. Spend ten minutes on it until you know it with your eyes closed.

oo meen**ya**	*I have*
oo vas	*you have*
oo neev**o**, oo nee**yo**	*he has, she has*
oo nas	*we have*
oo neekh	*they have*

4 Saying 'you'

Russian has two words for you. If you know one person well, or are speaking to a child, use ti; if you are being polite and formal to one person use vi or if you are speaking to more than one person, also use vi. In **Fast Russian with Elisabeth Smith** you only use vi.

5 Doing things

Did you notice that when you say *I*, *we* or *you* in Russian the ending of the verb changes? Here are the verbs you came across in the dialogue. Have another look at them. They are not for learning. You have done that already.

rabotat' *to work*	
ya rab**o**tayu	*I work*
mi rab**o**taeem	*we work*
vi rab**o**taeetee	*you work*

yekhat' *to travel*	
ya **ye**doo	*I travel*
mi **ye**deem	*we travel*
vi **ye**deetee	*you travel*

6 V: in, at, to

As you saw in the **New words** the Russian letter v (va)/f can mean *in*, *at*, *to* and sometimes even *on*, as in *on holiday* – v **o**tpooskee. That's the easy bit. Unfortunately, after a v the ending of the following word changes. So Maskv**a** becomes Maskv**oo** (*to Moscow*) and *bank* becomes bankye *(at the bank)*. But don't worry about it. This is just for knowing, not for learning! You'll pick it up as you go along.

7 Asking questions

'Vi tozhe'. *You, too*. 'Vi tozhe?' *You, too?* You simply use your voice to turn a statement into a question. Easy!

Learn by heart

🔊 CD1, tr 6

Don't be tempted to skip this exercise because it reminds you of school... If you want to speak, not stumble, saying a few lines by heart does the trick!

Learn **Meenya zavoot** by heart after you have filled in the gaps with your personal, or any, information.

Example: Meen**ya** zav**oo**t Colin Bell.
Ya eez Londana.

When you know the seven lines by heart, go over them again until you can say them out loud fluently and fairly fast. Can you beat 40 seconds?

Meenya zavoot

Meen**ya** zav**oo**t ....(NAME)

Ya eez ....(PLACE)

Ya rab**o**tayu v b**a**nkee ....

Oo meen**ya** bal'shaya kvart**ee**ra. An**a** d**o**roga st**o**eet.

V m**a**rtee ya bil/bil**a** v ....(PLACE)

F seenteebr**ye** mi **ye**deem v ....(PLACE)

Vi t**o**zhe?

Let's speak Russian

I shall give you ten English sentences and you'll put them into Russian. Always speak out loud. After each one check the answer at the bottom of the page. Tick it if you got it right. If you have the recording, listen to check the answers to **Let's speak Russian**.

1 I am called Tom Walker.
2 Are you from London?
3 Yes, I am from London.
4 I have a girlfriend in Florida.
5 We are going to Moscow.
6 Do you have a Mercedes?
7 No, unfortunately (not).
8 We have a house in Novgorod.
9 There is more money in the bank.
10 Is the job boring?

Well, how many did you get right? If you are not happy, do it again! Now here are some questions in Russian and you are going to answer in Russian. Answer the next five questions with da and ya.

11 Vi eez Manch**ye**s'teera?
12 Oo vas dom v L**o**ndanee?
13 Vi **ye**deetee v Maskv**oo**?
14 Vi rab**o**taeetee bees komp'**yu**tera?
15 Vi bilee **v** Br**ee**stolee pa b**ee**znisoo?

And now answer the next five questions with da and ya, mi or oo nas.

16 Vi **ye**deetee v N**o**vgarat?
17 Oo vas meest**a** 9a ee 9b?
18 Oo vas **o**tpoosk v apr**ye**lee?
19 Vi b**i**lee tree g**o**da v L**o**ndanee?
20 Oo vas seech**ya**s bol'shi d**ye**neek?

WEEK 1

Answers

1 Meenya zavoot Tom Walker.
2 Vi eez Londana?
3 Da, ya eez Londana.
4 Oo meenya padrooga v Flareedee.
5 Mi yedeem v Maskvoo.
6 Oo vas Meerseedes?
7 Nyet, k sazhilyeneeyu.
8 Oo nas dom v Novgaradee.
9 V bankee bol'shi dyeneek.
10 Rabota skoochnaya?
11 Da, ya eez Manchyes'teera.
12 Da, oo meenya dom v Londanee.
13 Da, ya yedoo v Maskvoo.
14 Da, ya rabotayu bees komp'yutera.
15 Da, ya bil/bila v Breestolee pa beeznisoo.
16 Da, ya yedoo v Novgarat.
17 Da, oo nas meesta 9a ee 9b.
18 Da, oo nas otpoosk v apryelee.
19 Da, mi bilee tree goda v Londanee.
20 Da, oo nas seechyas bol'shi dyeneek.

Well, what was your score? If you ticked all of them.

12

Let's speak more Russian

🔊 CD1, tr 8

Here are some optional exercises. They may stretch the 45 minutes a day by 15 minutes. But the extra practice will be worth it.

And always remember: near enough is good enough!

In your own words

This exercise will teach you to express yourself freely. Use only the words you have learned so far.

Tell me in your own words that...

1 you are from Manchester
2 unfortunately your work is boring
3 you have a son and daughter
4 you work in a university
5 you have a house in Birmingham
6 you are going to Moscow
7 you have a friend in London
8 Yalta is a very beautiful town
9 you are on holiday
10 a big flat in New York is very expensive

Answers

1 Ya eez Manch**ye**s'tyera.
2 K sazhil**ye**neeyu rab**o**ta sk**oo**chnaya.
3 Oo myen**ya** sin ee doch.
4 Ya rab**o**tayu v ooneevyeerseet**ye**tee.
5 Oo meen**ya** dom v Beermeeng**ye**mee.
6 Ya **ye**doo v Maskv**oo**.
7 Oo meen**ya** padr**oo**ga v L**o**ndanee.
8 Y**a**lta **o**cheen' kras**ee**viiy g**o**rat.
9 Oo meen**ya o**tpoosk.
10 Bal'sh**a**ya kvart**ee**ra v Nyu Y**o**rke st**o**eet **o**cheen' d**o**raga.

Let's speak Russian – fast and fluently

🔊 CD1, tr 9

No more stuttering and stumbling! Get out the stopwatch and time yourself with this fluency practice. Some of the English is in 'Russian-speak' to help you.

Translate each section and check if it is correct. Then cover up the answers and say the three or four sentences fast! Try to say each group of sentences in less than 30 seconds.

Good morning. I am going to Moscow. You too?
No, I work in New York – in a bank. Now I am going to Yalta on business.
My wife is from Novgorod.
I have in September holiday – without telephone.

Dobraye **oo**tra. Ya **ye**doo v Maskv**oo**. Vi t**o**zhe?
Nyet, ya rab**o**tayu v Nyu Y**o**rke – v b**a**nkee. Seech**a**s ya **ye**doo v **Ya**ltoo pa b**ee**znisoo.
M**a**ya zhin**a** eez N**o**vgarada.
Oo meen**ya** v seenteebr**ye o**tpoosk – bees teeleef**o**na.

Hello. Who you?
Me they call John. I have a girlfriend, Tanya. She programmer.
In bank in Moscow.
I work in university. The work there very good.

Zdr**a**stvooiytee. Kto vi?
Meen**ya** zav**oo**t John. Oo meen**ya** padr**oo**ga, T**a**nya. An**a** pragram**ee**st.
V b**a**nkee v Maskv**ye**.
Ya rab**o**tayu v oonee**ve**erseet**ye**tee. Rab**o**ta tam khar**o**shaya.

I have flat in Moscow. Costs very expensive.
We were two years in Moscow. Moscow very beautiful town.
Now we in London.
Excuse me, little minute (just a moment), please. My wife rings.

Oo meen**ya** kvart**ee**ra v Maskv**ye**. St**o**eet **o**cheen' d**o**raga.
Mi bil**ee** dva g**o**da v Maskv**ye**. M**a**skva **o**cheen' kras**ee**viiy g**o**rat.
Seech**a**s mi v L**o**ndanee.
Eezveen**ee**tee, meen**oo**tachkoo, pazhal**oo**sta. M**aya** zhin**a** zvan**ee**t.

Test your progress

This is your only written exercise. You'll be amazed at how easy it is! Translate the 20 sentences without looking at the previous pages. The bits in brackets help you with the difference between English and Russian.

(Please note: write the words straight: don't alternate bold type and light to show where the word is stressed. It would take you forever!)

1 They call me (I am called) Frank Lukas.
2 Hello, we (are) Viktor and Olga.
3 I (am) also from Omsk.
4 In October I was in Moscow.
5 We were three years in America.
6 London is very expensive.
7 Excuse me, please. Where (do) you work?
8 Are you working in Manchester?
9 (Are) you Viktor Izmailov from Tomsk?
10 (The) flat in Novgorod is very big.
11 Little minute (just a moment), please, by me (I have) more money.
12 There there is (a) telephone? No, unfortunately not.
13 I (am) in Yalta without (my) son.
14 (Is) (the) company big?
15 (Is) (a) Mercedes expensive?
16 In April London (is) very beautiful.
17 By him (he has) in (the) travel agency (a) girlfriend.
18 Unfortunately (the) work (is) very boring.
19 (The) job is very good, but (a) holiday is better.
20 My daughter telephones always.

When you have finished look up the answers in the **Answers** section and mark your work. Then enter your result on the **Progress chart** at the front of the book. If your score is higher than 80% you'll have done very well indeed!

Week 2
Day-by-Day Guide

Forty-five minutes a day – but a little extra will step up your progress!

Day one
- Read **In Saint Petersburg**.
- Listen to/Read **f Sankt-Peeteerboorgee**.
- Listen to/Read the **New words**. Learn 20 easy ones.

Day two
- Repeat **f Sankt-Peeteerboorgee** and the **New words**.
- Go over **Pronunciation**.
- Learn the harder **New words**.
- Use the **Flash words** to help you.

Day three
- Learn all the **New words** until you know them well.
- Read and learn the **Good news grammar**.

Day four
- Cut out and learn the **Flash sentences**.
- Listen to/Read **Learn by heart**.

Day five
- Listen to/Read **Let's speak Russian**.
- Go over **Learn by heart**.

Day six
- Listen to/Read **Let's speak more Russian** (optional).
- Listen to/Read **Let's speak Russian – fast and fluently** (optional).
- Translate **Test your progress**.

Day seven – This is a study-free day!

In Saint Petersburg

In Saint Petersburg Tom and Kate check in to a hotel. Later they go to a café for something to drink.

Kate Good day. By you (do you have) room for two, for one night? Costs not too expensive?

Hotelier Yes, by us (we have) room with a bath and shower... but shower it is necessary to repair, it does not work.

Tom Where is room?

Hotelier On tenth floor.

Kate How much does it cost?

Hotelier Only 500 roubles per person, but credit cards we do not accept! Breakfast from eight o'clock to nine.

Tom Well... we want room. But is it possible to have breakfast at 7.45? By us (we have) excursion tomorrow at 8.15.

Kate And I have question. Where is it possible to drink coffee or tea? Where here café?

Hotelier Café from here is near, to the left, then to the right 30 metres, then straight on.

(In the café...)

Waiter I am listening you (What can I get you?).

Kate For us coffee without sugar and tea with milk.

Waiter Is it all? By us (we have) sandwiches with cheese and with ham.

Tom One sandwich with cheese and one with ham, please.

Tom Cheese terrible.

Kate But ham good.

Tom Table too small.

Kate But toilets very clean.

Tom My tea cold.

Kate But waiter very beautiful (handsome).

Tom Bill, please.

Waiter Fifty roubles.

F Sankt-Peeteerboorgee

◄)) CD1, tr 10

In Saint Petersburg Tom and Kate check in to a hotel. Later they go to a café for something to drink.

Kate   Dobriiy dyen'. Oo vas yes't' nomeer na dvaeekh, na adnoo noch? Stoeet nee sleeshkam doraga?

Hotelier Da, oo nas nomeer s vanay ee s dooshim... a doosh nada atreemanteeravat', on nye rabotaeet.

Tom   Gdye nomeer?

Hotelier Na desyatam itazhe.

Kate   Skol'ka stoeet?

Hotelier Tol'ka peet'sot rooblyeiy na cheelavyeka, no kreedeeetniee kartachkee mi nye preeneemaeem! Zaftrak s vas'mee cheesof da deeveeeatee.

Tom   Noo... mi khateem nomeer. A mozhna zaftrakat' f syem' sorak pyat'? Oo nas ikskoorseeya zaftra v voseem' peetnatsat.

Kate   Ee o meenya vapros. Gdye mozhna peet' kofee eelee chyaiy? Gdye z'dyes' kafe?

Hotelier Kafe atsyuda bleeska, nalyeva, patom naprava treetsat myetraf, patom pryama.

(In the café...)

Waiter   Slooshayu vas.

Kate   Nam kofee bees sakhara ee chyaiy s malakom.

Waiter   Eta fsyo? Oo nas bootibrodi s siram ee s veetcheenoiy.

Tom   Adeen bootibrot s siram ee adeen s veetcheenoiy, pazhaloosta.

Tom   Sir oozhasniiy.

Kate   A veetcheena kharoshaya.

Tom   Stol sleeshkam maleenkeeiy.

Kate   A tooalyeti ocheen' cheestiee.

Tom   Moiy chyaiy khalodniy.

Kate   A afeetsiant kraseeviiy.

Tom   Shshyot, pazhaloosta.

Waiter   Peedeesyat rooblyiey.

New words

🔊 CD1, tr 11

dobriiy dyen' *good day*

yes't' *there is/is there*

nomeer na dva**ee**kh *room for two (i.e. double room)*

na *for, on*

na ad**noo** noch *for one night*

nye *not*

slee**sh**kam *too (as in too much)*

s, z *with, from*

s **va**naiy *with a bathroom*

doosh (z **doo**shim) *shower (with a shower)*

a *and, but*

n**a**da *it is necessary*

atreemant**ee**ravat' *to repair*

on *it/he*

nee rab**o**taeet *does not work*

na des**ya**tam itazhe *on the tenth floor*

sk**o**l'ka *how much/how many*

t**o**l'ka *only*

peets**o**t *500*

roobl**ee**, roobl**yeiy** *rouble(s)*

na cheelav**ye**ka *for a person (per person)*

kreed**ee**tniee k**a**rtachkee *credit cards*

preeneem**a**eem *we accept*

z**a**ftrak *breakfast*

s vas'm**ee** cheesof *from eight hours (from eight o'clock)*

do, da *until*

d**ye**veet'/deevee**tee** *nine*

noo... *well...*

mi khat**ee**m *we want*

m**o**zhna *it is possible*

z**a**ftrakat' *to have breakfast*

syem' s**o**rak pyat' *7.45*

iks**koo**rseeya *excursion*

z**a**ftra *tomorrow*

v**o**seem' peetn**a**tsat *8.15*

vap**ro**s *question*

k**o**fee *coffee*

eelee *or*

chy**a**iy *tea*

peet'/ya p'yu *to drink/I drink*

z'dyes' *here*

kaf**e** *café*

ats**yu**da *from here*

bl**ee**ska *close, near*

nal**ye**va *to the left, on the left*

napr**a**va *to the right, on the right*

tr**ee**tsat m**ye**traf *30 metres*

pat**o**m *then, next*

pr**ya**ma *straight on*

sl**oo**shayu *I listen*

vi/vas *you*

nam *for us*

s**a**khar/s**a**khara *sugar*

malak**o**/malak**o**m *milk*

fsyo *all, everything*

bootirbr**o**t/bootirbr**o**di *sandwich/sandwiches*

sir/s**i**ram *cheese*

veetcheena/veetcheenoiy *ham*
oozhasniiy *terrible*
stol *table*
maleen'keeiy/maleen'kaya *small*
tooalyeti *toilets*

cheestiee *clean*
khalodniy *cold*
afeetsiant *waiter*
shshyot *bill*
peedeesyat *50*

> **TOTAL NEW WORDS: 67**
> ...only 239 words to go!

Some useful extras
Tsifri *(numerals)*

adeenatsat'	11	dveenatsat'	12	treenatsat'	13
cheetirnatsat'	14	peetnatsat'	15	shisnatsat'	16
seemnatsat'	17	vaseemnatsat	18	deeveetnatsat'	19
dvatsat'	20	treetsat'	30	sorak	40
peedeesyat	50	shiz'deesyat	60	syemdeesyat	70
voseemdeesyat	80	deeveenosta	90	sto	100
dvyes'tee	200	treesta	300	cheetireesta	400
peetsot	500	shisot	600	tiseechya	1000

You join numbers just like in English: *23* = dvatsat' tree;
35 = treetsat pyat'.

Vryemya *(telling the time)*

cheesi *clock*
f katoram cheesoo? *at what time?*
f tree cheesa *at three o'clock*
(f) syem' treetsat' (at) 7.30
chyas *hour*
needyelya *week*
got *year*

tree cheesa *it is three o'clock*
v dva cheesa *at two o'clock*
f pyat cheesof *at five o'clock*
meenoota *minute*
dyen' *day*
myeseets *month*

Good news grammar

◀) CD1, tr 12

1 Doing things

In Week 1 you learned how to say *I, you, we... work* or *travel*.

Now let's complete the list with *he, she, it* and *they... work* or *are working*.

Bar**ee**s rab**o**taeet. On rab**o**taeet.
Ol'ga rab**o**taeet. An**a** rab**o**taeet.
Teelee**fo**n rab**o**taeet. On
   rab**o**taeet.
Bar**ee**s ee Ol'ga rab**o**tayut. An**ee**
   rab**o**tayut.

Boris works. He is working.
Olga works. She is working.
The telephone works. It is
   working.
Boris and Olga work. They
   are working.

So it's **-eet** for one person and **-yut** for more than one. And if you want to use the basic form, i.e. *to work*, it's rab**o**tat' (with an apostrophe at the end).

2 'To want' and 'to be able to/can'

Here are two important verbs which you'll use all the time. Unfortunately, they don't behave as well as rab**o**tat'. I have put them into gift boxes for you so you won't forget. Spend five minutes on each. Use *want* instead of *would like*. It does not sound at all rude in Russian.

---

khatyet' *want*
ya khach**u**   *I want*
vi khat**ee**tee   *you want*
mi khat**ee**m   *we want*
on, an**a**, an**o**   *he, she, it*
   kh**o**cheet   *wants*
an**ee** khat**ya**t   *they want*

moch' *can*
ya mag**oo**   *I can*
vi m**o**zhite   *you can*
mi m**o**zhim   *we can*
on, an**a**, an**o**   *he, she, it*
   m**o**zhit   *can*
an**ee** m**o**goot   *they can*

---

3 *Nada*: the 'necessary' and *mozhna*: the 'possible'

These are two very useful words. Remember when Olga said that the shower needed repairing:

> Nada atreemant**ee**ravat'... *It is necessary to repair...*

And then Tom wondered if they could have breakfast:

> M**o**zhna **za**ftrakat'? *Is it possible to have breakfast?*

When you use n**a**da and m**o**zhna you'll carry on with the basic verb – just like in English. *It is necessary/possible to work/drink*: nada/mozhna rab**o**tat'/peet', etc.

4 Word order: very relaxed!

We don't accept credit cards could be either: kreed**ee**tniee kartachkee mi nee preeneem**a**eem or mi nee preeneem**a**eem kreed**ee**tniye kartachkee. Take your pick!

5 *Nyet* and *nye*

Everyone knows nyet means *no*! Its 'brother' nye (*not*) is used when you are not doing something.

I don't work.	Ya nye rab**o**tayu.
He's not working.	On nye rab**o**taeet.

6 ...and now for the bad news: endings

There are three types of nouns in Russian: masculine, feminine and neuter. You can often identify which is which by the ending – usually a *consonant* (masculine), an **a** (feminine) or an **o** (neuter). The trouble starts when you use a noun in a sentence. Take sir: *cheese*. Take *bread with cheese*: bootirbrot s siram. Sir changes to siram. Adjectives and numbers behave equally badly: *new* could be: n**o**viy, n**o**vim, n**o**vaya and more! But don't despair. You'll pick them up as you go along.

Let's speak Russian

◀》 CD1, tr 13

Now let's practise what you have learned. I'll give you ten English sentences and you say them in Russian – out loud! If you have the recording, listen to check the answers. Tick each sentence if you got it right. Unless you got all ten correct, do the exercise again.

1 We would like a double room.
2 Unfortunately, it is too expensive.
3 Breakfast is at what time?
4 The telephone does not work.
5 We want sandwiches.
6 Do you also have tea?
7 Where is the café, left or right?
8 The toilets are not clean.
9 Can I please have the bill?
10 Tomorrow I go to London at nine o'clock.

Now answer in Russian. Use da and mi for the ones on the left and nyet and ya for the ones on the right.

11 Vi khateetee yekhat' v Maskvoo?
12 Oo vas z'dyes' teeleefon?
13 Vi khateetee yes't' (*to eat*) v voseem cheesof?
14 Vi mozhitee rabotat' zaftra?
15 Vi khateetee nomeer?

Now answer the last two using the words in brackets.

16 Gdye z'dyes' kafe? (bleeska, atsyuda)
17 F katoram cheesoo vi khateetee yes't'? (v shes't' sorak pyat)

Answers

1 Mi khateem nomeer na dvaeekh.
2 K sazhilyeneeyu eta stoeet sleeshkam doraga.
3 Zaftrak v katoram cheesoo?
4 Teeleefon nye rabotaeet.
5 Mi khateem bootirbrodi.
6 A chyaiy oo vas yes't'?
7 Gdye kafe, nalyeva eelee naprava?
8 Tooalyeti nee cheestiee.
9 Shshyot, pazhaloosta.
10 Zaftra ya v Londanee v dyeveet cheesof.
11 Da, mi khateem yekhat' v Maskvoo.
12 Da, oo nas z'dyes' yes't' teeleefon.
13 Nyet, ya nee khachu yes't' v voseem cheesof.
14 Nyet, ya nee magoo rabotat' zaftra.
15 Nyet, ya nee khachu nomeer.
16 Kafe bleeska atsyuda.
17 Ya khachu yes't' f shes't' sorak pyat.

Let's speak more Russian

◄)) CD1, tr 14

Here are the two optional exercises. Remember, they may stretch the 45 minutes a day by 15 minutes. But the extra practice will be worth it.

In your own words

This exercise will teach you to express yourself freely. Use only the words you have learned so far.

Tell me in your own words that...

1 you want to know if an en suite double room is available
2 you want to know the price of the room for one night
3 you would like breakfast at 7.30
4 you would like to know where you can have a tea or a coffee
5 you have an excursion to Novgorod at 8.45
6 you want to know if the café is close by. Is it to the left and then straight ahead, 100 metres?
7 you want tea without sugar, a sandwich with cheese and a sandwich with ham

Tell me...

8 what you don't like about the café (awful tea, small table, dirty toilets)
9 that Kate says the waiter is good looking (Kate gavar**eet**, shto... *Kate says that...*)
10 that the bill is 80 roubles

Answers

1 Oo vas yes't' nomeer na dva**ee**kh s v**a**naiy ee z d**oo**shim?
2 Sk**ol**'ka st**o**eet n**o**meer na adn**oo** noch?
3 M**o**zhna zafrakat' v syem' tr**ee**tsat'?
4 Gdye m**o**zhna peet' chyaiy **ee**lee k**o**fee?
5 Oo nas iksk**oo**rseeya v N**o**vgarat v v**o**seem' s**o**rak pyat.
6 Kaf**e** ats**yu**da bl**ee**ska? Kaf**e** nal**ye**va, pat**o**m naprava ee pr**ya**ma sto m**ye**traf?
7 Nam chyaiy bees s**a**khara, bootirbr**o**t s s**i**ram ee bootirbr**o**t s veecheen**oiy**, pazhaloosta.
8 Chyaiy oozh**a**sniiy, stol sl**ee**shkam m**a**leen'keeiy ee tooal**ye**ti nye **o**cheen' ch**ee**stiee.
9 Kate gavar**ee**t, shto afeetsi**a**nt kras**ee**viiy.
10 Shshyot – v**o**seem'deesyat roobl**yeiy**.

Let's speak Russian – fast and fluently

◀) CD1, tr 15

Translate each section and check if it is correct. Then cover up the answers and say the three or four sentences as quickly as you can. Try to say each group of sentences in less than 30 seconds. Some of the English is in Russian-speak to help you.

Good evening. Do you have a room with bath?
700 roubles per person – too expensive.
I want room with shower.
How much costs breakfast?

Dobriiy vyecheer. Oo vas yes't' nomeer s vanaiy?
Seemsot rooblyeiy na cheelavyeka – sleeshkam doraga.
Ya khachu nomeer z dooshim.
Skol'ka stoeet zaftrak?

Bank from here very near, straight ahead, then right 20 metres.
Tomorrow at five o'clock we are going to Yalta. Do you also want to go to Yalta?
Is it possible to have breakfast at ten o'clock?

Bank atsyuda ocheen' bleeska, pryama, patom naprava dvatsat myetraf.
Zaftra f pyat cheesof mi yedeem v Yaltoo. Vi tozhe khateetee yekhat' v Yaltoo?
Mozhna zaftrakat v dyeseet' cheesof?

The room costs very expensive. Do you have a credit card?
My breakfast – cold and coffee – awful.
The bill, please. One hundred and five roubles.

Nomeer stoeet ocheen' doraga. Oo vas yes't' kreedeetnaya kartachka?
Moiy zaftrak khalodniy ee kofee oozhasniiy.
Shshyot, pazhaloosta. Sto pyat rooblyeiy.

Learn by heart

🔊 CD1, tr 16

Choose one of these to fill in the gaps: ma**ee**m moozhim *husband*, ma**yeiy** zhin**o**iy *wife*, ma**ee**m dr**oo**gam *friend*, ma**yeiy** padr**oo**gaiy *girlfriend*. Try to say it in under one minute.

Oo meenya mala dyeneek, no…

Oo meen**ya** m**a**la* d**y**eneek, no ya khach**u o**tpoosk v m**a**ee.

Ya khach**u ye**khat' f Sankt-Peeteerb**oo**rk s…

Ya khach**u** f Sankt-Peeteerb**oo**rgee peet' mn**o**ga** shamp**a**nskava

ee yes't' bootirbr**o**di. **E**ta vazm**o**zhna***? Da, **e**ta need**o**raga st**o**eet.

Tol'ka d**y**es**ee**t' t**i**seech roobl**yeiy** na cheelav**y**eka, ee oo meen**ya** yes't'

kreed**ee**tnaya k**a**rtachka…

*mala: *a little* **mnoga: *a lot, many* ***vazmozhna: *it is possible*

Test your progress

Translate these sentences into Russian and write them out. See what you can remember without looking at the previous pages. (Remember. Don't highlight the part of the word which is stressed.)

1 I drink a lot of champagne.
2 How much is (costs) breakfast, please?
3 Is there a travel agency here?
4 Do you have a table? At 7.15?
5 I would like to drink (some) coffee.
6 My holiday in Florida was better.
7 Where is there a good hotel?
8 Can I have the telephone bill, please?
9 We were in Saint Petersburg in May.
10 My house is too big.
11 At what time are you in Moscow tomorrow?
12 I am there from eight until five.
13 Excuse me, please. Where are the toilets, straight ahead?
14 We want to travel to Oslo in January, but it is too cold.
15 Does that cost more money?
16 Tomorrow where are you at 10.30?
17 It's terrible. The (hotel) room is very expensive.
18 Is it possible to drink coffee here now? Do you have seats?
19 We have a small house in America, but it is very expensive.
20 Goodbye, we are going to Yalta.

Check your answers and work out your score. Now enter your result on the **Progress chart** in the front of the book. If it is above 70% you have done very well.

Week 3
Day-by-day guide

Study for 45 minutes a day – but there are no penalties for doing more!

Day one
- Read **Let's go shopping**.
- Listen to/Read **Mi dyelaeem pakoopkee**.
- Listen to/Read the **New words**, then learn some of them.

Day two
- Repeat **Mi dyelaeem pakoopkee** and the **New words**.
- Learn all the **New words**. Use the **Flash cards**.

Day three
- Test yourself on all the **New words** – boring perhaps, but you are over halfway already.
- Read and learn the **Good news grammar**.
- Go over the **Good news grammar**.

Day four
- Listen to/Read **Learn by heart**.
- Cut out and learn the ten **Flash sentences**.

Day five
- Listen to/Read **Spot the keys**.
- Listen to/Read **Let's speak Russian**.

Day six
- Go over **Learn by heart**.
- Have a quick look at **New words**, Weeks 1–3. You now know over 200 words! Well, more or less.
- Listen to/Read **Let's speak more Russian** (optional).
- Listen to/Read **Let's speak Russian – fast and fluently** (optional).
- Translate **Test your progress**.

Day seven – Enjoy your day off!

Let's go shopping

Tom and Kate are staying in Moscow. Kate plans some shopping but Tom has other ideas.

Kate Well, today for us it is necessary to do shopping. First we go to centre of town on bus.

Tom But weather bad. (It is) Cold. And on television much sport. At 12.30 goes (is on) golf...

Kate Sorry, but for us it is necessary (to go) to bank, to post office for stamps, to chemist's, to dry cleaner's and to supermarket.

Tom Well, golf not possible to watch... perhaps football at three o'clock. Is that all?

Kate No, for us it is necessary also (to go) to department store for new suitcase and to hairdresser's. And I want also (to go) to jewellery shop and to shop of souvenirs.

Tom Good grief! Shops open until what time?

Kate Until six or until eight, it seems.

Tom Ah, football also not possible to watch... perhaps tennis at 8.30...

(Later...)

Kate It seems, I too many presents bought. Bottle of champagne, tin of caviar, Russian dolls, chocolate.

Tom No problem! For us it is necessary to buy many presents. But what there, in big bag? Is it for me?

Kate And yes and no. I was in jewellery shop, then in department store. In jewellery shop I saw brooch. It is amber brooch. Splendid, isn't it true? Shop assistant was very pleasant and so handsome as Tom Cruise.

Tom Who such (who is) Tom Cruise? And how much costs brooch?

Kate A little expensive... 600 roubles.

Tom What?... Crazy!

Kate But here is T-shirt. It costs not very expensive. And here's English newspaper... and on television now is going (is on) tennis, isn't it true?

Mi dyelaeem pakoopkee

🔊 CD1, tr 17

Tom and Kate are staying in Moscow. Kate plans some shopping but Tom has other ideas.

Kate   Noo, seevodnya nam nada dyelat' pakoopkee. Snachyala mi yedeem f tsentr gorada na avtoboosee.

Tom   No pagoda plakhaya. Kholadna. Ee po teeleeveezaroo mnoga sporta. V dveenatsat treetsat eedyot gol'f...

Kate   Ezveenee, no nam nada v bank, na pochtoo za markamee, v aptyekoo, f kheemcheestkoo ee f soopeermarkeet.

Tom   Noo, gol'f neel'zya smatryet'... mozhit bit' footbol f tree cheesa. Eta fsyo?

Kate   Nyet, nam nada tozhe v ooneeveermak za novim cheemadanam ee f pareekmakheerskooyu. Ee ya khachu v yuveeleerniy magazeen ee v magazeen sooveeneeraf.

Tom   Bozhe moiy! Magazeeni atkriti da kakova chyasa?

Kate   Da shes't'ee eelee da vas'mee, kazhitsa.

Tom   Akh, foodbol tozhe neel'zya smatryet'... mozhit bit' tenees v voseem' treetsat'...

(Later...)

Kate   Kazhetsa, ya sleeshkam mnoga padarkaf koopeela. Bootilkoo shampanskava, bankoo eekri, matryoshkee, shikalat.

Tom   Nyet prablyem! Nam nada koopeet' mnoga padarkaf. A shto tam v balshoiy soomkee? Eta dlya meenya?

Kate   Ee da ee nyet. Ya bila v yuveeleernam magazeenee, patom v ooneeveermagee. V yuveeleernam magazeenee ya ooveedeela broshkoo. Eta yantarnaya broshka. Preekrasnaya, nye pravda lee? Pradavyets bil ocheen' preeyatniiy ee takoiy zhe krasaveets, kak Tom Cruise.

Tom   Kto takoiy Tom Cruise? Ee skol'ka stoeet broshka?

Kate   Neemnoshka doraga. Shisot (600) rooblyeiy.

Tom   Shto? S ooma sashla!

Kate   No vot foodbolka. Stoeet nye ocheen' doraga. A vot angleeskaya gazyeta... a po teeleeveezaroo seechyas eedyot tenees, nye pravda lee?

New words

◀) CD1, tr 18

Learn the **New words** in half the time using the **Flash cards** at the back of the book. There are 22 to start you off.

seev**o**dnya *today*
d**ye**lat' *to do*
pak**oo**pkee *the shopping*
snach**ya**la *first*
tsentr *centre*
aft**o**boos/aft**o**boosee *bus*
pag**o**da *weather*
plakh**a**ya *bad*
kh**o**ladna *cold*
po, pa *on, along, according to*
teeleev**ee**zar/teeleev**ee**zaroo
   television
sp**o**rt/sp**o**rta/sp**o**rtoo *sport*
eed**yo**t *(he, she) it goes,*
   is going
eezveen**ee** *I am sorry (informal)*
p**o**chta/p**o**chtoo *post office*
za *for, behind, beyond*
m**a**rkee/m**a**rkamee *stamps*
apt**ye**ka/apt**ye**koo *chemist's*
kheemch**ee**stka/kheemch**ee**stkoo
   drycleaner's
soopeerm**a**rkeet *supermarket*
neel'z**ya** *it is not possible, one*
   may not
smatr**ye**t' *to watch*
m**o**zhit bit' *perhaps*
f tree cheesa *at three o'clock*
ooneeveerm**a**g/ooneeveerm**a**gee
   department store
n**o**viy/n**o**vim *new*

cheemad**a**n/cheemad**a**nam
   suitcase
pareekm**a**kheerskaya/
   pareekm**a**kheerskooyu
   hairdresser's
yuvel**ee**rniy *jewellery*
magaz**ee**n/magaz**ee**nee *shop/*
   shops
sooveen**ee**ri/sooveen**ee**raf
   souvenirs
B**o**zhe moiy! *Good grief!*
   (lit: God my!)
atkr**i**ti *open (plural form)*
da kak**o**va ch**ya**sa? *until when?*
k**a**zhitsa *it seems, I think/believe*
t**e**nees *tennis*
mn**o**ga *many*
koop**ee**la *(I) bought*
bootilk**oo** shamp**a**nskava *bottle (of)*
   champagne
shamp**a**nskaye *champagne*
pad**a**rkee/pad**a**rkaf *presents*
b**a**nka/b**a**nkoo *tin, jar*
eek**ra**/eek**ri** *caviar*
matr**yo**shka/matr**yo**shkee *Russian*
   doll/dolls
shikal**a**t *chocolate*
nyet prabl**ye**m! *no problem!*
koop**ee**t'/koop**ee**la *to buy/she*
   bought
shto *what, that*

soomka, soomkee/pakyeteek
  bag
dlya meenya *for me*
ooveedeet'/ooveedeela *to see/she
  saw*
broshka/broshkoo *brooch*
yantarnaya *amber*
preekrasnaya *splendid*
nye pravda lee *isn't it?*
pradavyets *shop assistant*
preeyatniiy *pleasant*

takoiy zhe ... kak *just as ... as*
krasaveets *handsome fellow*
kto takoiy... ? *Who is... ?*
neemnoshka *a little*
s ooma sashla *crazy! (to a man one
  would say:* **s ooma sashol**)
vot *here (there) is/are*
foodbolka *T-shirt*
angleeskaya/**A**ngleeya,
  Anglee-ee *English/England*
gazyeta *newspaper*

> **TOTAL NEW WORDS: 67**
> **...only 172 words to go!**

More extras
Tsveeta *(colours)*

byeliiy	*white*	zeelyoniiy	*green*
chyorniiy	*black*	aranzhiviiy	*orange*
krasniiy	*red*	rozaviiy	*pink*
seeneey	*blue*	syeriiy	*grey*
zholtiiy	*yellow*	kareechneeviiy	*brown*

Spot the keys

◀》 CD1, tr 19

By now you can say many things in Russian. But what happens if you ask a question and don't understand the answer – hitting you at the speed of a machine gun? The smart way is not to panic, but to listen out for the words you know. Any familiar words which you pick up will provide you with key words – clues to what the other person is saying.

If you have the recording listen to the dialogue. If you don't – read on. You are trying to ask the way to the post office...

You   Eezveeneetee, pazhaloosta, gdye pochta?

Answer   *Noo, eta nye tak prosta. Snachyala eedeetee* pryama
              da *slyedooshcheevapeereekryostka, tamgdyenakhodeetsa*
              balshoiy krasniiy dom. Patom nalyeva, *vi ooveedeetee*
              tam eeshshyo magazeeni. *Eeshshyopadalshye eedeetye*
              naprava. Viooveedeetee aptyekoo *naproteef pochti.*

Did you hear the key words? **pryama da – balshoiy krasniiy dom –
patom – nalyeva – magazeeni – aptyekoo – pochti.**

Good news grammar

◀))) CD1, tr 20

1 The past

This is easier than in French! Here's a very basic 'recipe:

- Take the basic form of the verb, say, rab**o**tat.
- Take off the t and add an I if you are talking about one male person (it could be Boris or yourself): Bar**ee**s rab**o**tal.
- Add la for one female person (it could be Tanya or you): T**a**nya rab**o**tala.
- Add lo for neuter nouns: rad**ee**a ne rabotalo (pronounced rab**o**tala).
- Add lee for *you* (vi) and everything that's more than one: *Boris and Tanya, we, they…* rab**o**talee.

Most important: learn all the sample phrases which are in the past.

2 *Nada, mozhna* and *neel'zya*

Remember n**a**da and m**o**zhna from Week 2? *It is necessary. It is possible.* Here's another one: neel'z**ya**: *it's forbidden*, so *it's not possible.*

These three are very useful when you want to say *can, can't* or *must*, because that's really what they express: *I can… for me it's possible. I can't… for me it's not possible. I must… for me it's necessary.*

So all you need to do now is to add: *for me, for you, for us,* etc. Here's the full list using n**a**da and *must buy* as an example:

mnye n**a**da koop**ee**t'	*for me it is necessary… I must buy*
vam n**a**da koop**ee**t'	*for you it is necessary… you must buy*
nam n**a**da koop**ee**t'	*for us it is necessary… we must buy*
yem**oo**/yeiy n**a**da koop**ee**t'	*for him/her it is necessary… he/she must buy*
eem n**a**da koop**ee**t'	*for them it is necessary… they must buy.*

So now you can mix and match. **Mnye mozhna koopeet:** *I can buy.*
Nam neel'zya rabotat: *We can't work.*

3 'To go': *eetee'* 'on foot' and *yekhat'* 'by transport'

We've put these two useful verbs in a box to help you remember them.

eetee'		yekhat'
ya eedoo	*I go*	ya yedoo
vi eedyotee	*you go*	vi yedeetee
on, ana eedyot	*he, she goes*	on, ana yedeet
mi eedyom	*we go*	mi yedeem
anee eedoot	*they go*	anee yedoot

Learn by heart

🔊 CD2, tr 1

Say these lines in under 50 seconds. The more expression you use the easier it will be to remember all the useful bits.

Seevodnya nam nada dyelat' pakoopkee – nyet prablyem!

No atkooda* yedeet aftoboos v magazeeni?

Akh, bozhe moiy! Kazhitsa, oo meenya mala dyeneek.

Mi koopeelee mnoga padarkaf: matryoshkee, broshkoo ee bankoo eekri.

Eta bila doroga: shessot rooblyeiy, no pradavyets bil ocheen' preeyatniy.

*atkooda: *from where*

Let's speak Russian

◀》 CD2, tr 2

Over to you. If you have the recording, listen to check your answers. Always answer out loud. Start with a ten-point warm-up. Say in Russian:

1 Now I am going to (the) post office.
2 Until what time (are the) shops open?
3 I am sorry, but that is too expensive.
4 From where bus goes to centre?
5 We bought souvenirs in Novgorod.
6 Can one buy caviar in the supermarket?
7 Shopping without money? No, but I have (a) credit card.
8 I everything bought in the department store.
9 We must watch the weather on television.
10 Good grief! The television doesn't work!

Answer the following using the words in brackets.

11 Oo vas yes't' **see**nee-ee foodb**o**lkee? (da, oo nas)
12 Vi koop**ee**lee m**a**rkee f soopeerm**a**rkeetee? (da, mi)
13 Vi rab**o**talee v b**a**nkee? (nyet, mi)
14 Vam n**a**da eet**ee** v d**ye**veet chees**o**f? (nyet, nam)
15 Oo vas mn**o**ga d**ye**neek? (nyet, oo nas, m**a**la)
16 Shto vi koop**ee**lee? Shikal**a**t **ee**lee shamp**a**nskaye? (shikal**a**t)
17 Kto smatr**ye**l foodb**o**l po teeleev**ee**zaroo? (ya)
18 Da kak**o**va chy**a**sa magaz**ee**nee atkr**i**ti? (vas'm**ee** chees**o**f)

Answers

1 Seechyas ya eedoo na pochtoo.
2 Magazeeni atkriti da kakova chyasa?
3 Ezveeneetee no eta sleeshkam doraga.
4 Atkooda aftoboos yedeet f tsentr?
5 Mi koopeelee sooveeneeri v Novgaradee.
6 Mozhna koopeet' eekroo f soopeermarkeetee?
7 Dyelat' pakoopkee bees dyeneek? Nyet, no oo meenya yes't' kreedeetnaya kartachka.
8 Ya fsyo koopeela f ooneeveermagee.
9 Nam nada smatryet' pagodoo po teeleeveezaroo.
10 Bozhe moiy! Teeleeveezar nee rabotaeet!
11 Da, oo nas yes't' seenee-ee foodbolkee.
12 Da, mi koopeelee markee f soopeermarkeetee.
13 Nyet, mi nee rabotalee v bankee.
14 Nyet, nam nee nada eetee f dyeveet cheesof.
15 Nyet, oo nas mala dyeneek.
16 Mi koopeelee (ya koopeel/ya koopeela) shikalat.
17 Ya smatryel/ya smatryela foodbol po teeleeveezaroo.
18 Da vas'mee (cheesof).

Let's speak more Russian

◀🔊 CD2, tr 3

Here are the two optional exercises. Remember, they may stretch the 45 minutes a day by 15 minutes. But the extra practice will be worth it.

In your own words

This exercise will teach you to express yourself freely. Use only the words you have learned so far.

Tell me in your own words that...

1 today you must go shopping
2 first you are going to the centre of town by bus
3 unfortunately you have little money, but you do have a credit card
4 you have to go to the supermarket to buy a bottle of champagne
5 then you have to go to the department store to buy Russian dolls
6 you bought caviar, coffee and chocolate in the supermarket
7 it was very expensive; it seems now you have little money
8 you watched the weather on television
9 the sandwiches cost 15 roubles; that was not expensive
10 you have bought too many presents

Answers

1 Seevodnya mnye nada dyelat' pakoopkee.
2 Snachyala ya yedoo f tsentr gorada na aftoboosee.
3 K sazhilyeneeu oo meenya mala dyeneek, no oo meenya kreedeetnaya kartachka.
4 Mnye nada v soopeermarkeet koopeet' bootilkoo shampanskava.
5 Patom mnye nada v ooneeveermak koopeet' matryoshkee.
6 Ya koopeel/koopeela eekroo, kofee ee shikalat f soopeermarkeetee.
7 Eta bila ocheen' doraga. Kazhitsa, seechyas oo meenya mala dyeneek.
8 Ya smatryel/smatryela pagodoo po teeleeveezaroo.
9 Bootirbrodi stoeelee peetnatsat rooblyeiy. Eta bila nyedoraga.
10 Ya sleeshkam mnoga podarkaf koopeel/koopeela.

Let's speak Russian – fast and fluently

🔊 CD2, tr 4

Translate each section and check if it is correct. Then cover up the answers and say the three or four sentences as quickly as you can. Some of the English is in 'Russian-speak' to help you.

Good grief! Is that an English newspaper?
Do you want to watch football or tennis?
Did you watch the sport on the television?

Bo*zhe moiy!* **E**ta angl**ee**skaya gaz**y**e*ta?*
Vi khat**ee**tee smatr**y**et' foodb**o**l **ee**lee t**e**nees?
Vi smatr**y**eli sport po teeleev**ee**zaroo?

From where bus goes to university?
Excuse me, are you going to the pharmacy?
Where can I buy stamps?
We must buy souvenirs in department store.

Atk**oo**da aft**o**boos eed**y**ot v ooneeveerseet**y**et?
Eezveen**ee**tee, vi eed**y**otee v apt**y**ekoo?
Gdye m**o**zhna koop**ee**t' mark**ee**?
Nam n**a**da koopit' sooveen**ee**ri v ooneeveerm**a**gee.

Today the weather is good.
I don't need to go at six o'clock.
Today you mustn't work. You must go shopping.

Seev**o**dnya pag**o**da khar**o**shaya.
Mnye nee n**a**da eet**ee** f shes't' chees**o**f.
Seev**o**dnya vam neel'**z**ya rab**o**tat'. Vam n**a**da d**y**elat' pak**oo**pkee.

Now say all the sentences in Russian without stopping and starting. Try to do it in under 90 seconds. If you are not happy with your result – just try once more.

Test your progress

Translate the following sentences into Russian and write them down.
Then check your answers and be amazed.

1 Where is (the) sales assistant?
2 Where is it possible to buy sandwiches?
3 When must you (go) to England today? At seven o'clock?
4 We saw that yesterday on television.
5 Now (the) shops (are) open, it seems.
6 Here there is (a) department store or supermarket?
7 Excuse me, are you also going to the post office?
8 Where did you buy (the) English newspaper?
9 Do you want coffee or tea?
10 The weather is bad today. It is not possible to go to Novgorod.
11 That is all? That was not expensive.
12 The stamps cost 15 roubles.
13 We accept credit cards.
14 Is 300 grams (of) cheese too much? No, no problem.
15 There is (a) new dry cleaner's near here.
16 Do you have (a) bag for my T-shirt, please?
17 I saw here (a) chemist's, it seems.
18 Good grief! (The) bus has broken down (isn't working) and (the)
    Mercedes also has broken down (isn't working)!
19 Did you see (the) T-shirt? Where did you buy it?
20 Five hundred roubles, but I have only dollars.

Remember to fill in the **Progress chart**. You are now halfway home!

Week 4

Day-by-day guide

Study for 45 minutes a day but if you are keen try 50... 55...!

Day one
- Read **We're going to the restaurant**.
- Listen to/Read **Mi eedyom v reestaran**.
- Read the **New words**. Learn the easy ones.

Day two
- Repeat the dialogue. Learn the harder **New words**.
- Cut out the **Flash words** to help you.

Day three
- Learn all the **New words** until you know them well.
- Read and learn the **Good news grammar**.

Day four
- Listen to/Read **Learn by heart**.
- Cut out and learn the ten **Flash sentences**.

Day five
- Listen to/Read **Spot the keys**.
- Read **Say it simply**.

Day six
- Listen to/Read **Let's speak Russian**.
- Listen to/Read **Let's speak more Russian** (optional).
- Listen to/Read **Let's speak Russian – fast and fluently** (optional).
- Translate **Test your progress**.

Day seven
Are you keeping your scores above 60%? In that case... have a good day off!

We're going to (the) restaurant

Tom and Kate are off to dinner with an important client. Will Kate be able to handle the infamous Edith?

Don't forget that the English is in 'Russian-speak' to help you get used to the way the language works.

Kate   Tom, someone rang. He did not say why. Number is on paper, by telephone. Some Boris…

Tom   Oh, yes, Boris Vadimovich, good customer of our firm. I him well know. Very pleasant person. By me meeting with him on Thursday. Very important matter.

Tom   *(On the phone...)* Hello, good morning, Boris Vadimovich… Speaks Tom Walker… Yes, thank you… yes, of course, it is possible… next week… of course… yes… very interesting… no, by us time there is… splendid… no, only for a few days… I understand… when?… at 8 o'clock… upstairs by exit, by door. Well, until Tuesday, thank you very much, goodbye.

Kate   What are we doing on Tuesday?

Tom   We are going to restaurant with Boris Vadimovich. Restaurant in centre behind church. He says, that restaurant new. Boris Vadimovich in Moscow for two days, with Edith and Peter Palmer from our firm.

Kate   I know Edith Palmer. She is boring and knows everything. She has a terrible dog. I think, that on Tuesday I will be ill. Heavy cold and everything hurts. The doctor necessary it will be to call…

Tom   Please, (one can't do that) thus it is not possible; it's not on. Boris Vadimovich is very important client.

Mi eedyom v reestaran

🔊 CD2, tr 5

Tom and Kate are off to dinner with an important client. Will Kate be able to handle the infamous Edith?

Kate Tom, kto-ta pazvaneel. On nee skazal, pacheemoo. Nomeer na boomagee, okala teeleefona. Kakoiy-ta Barees.

Tom Akh, da, Barees Vadeemaveech, kharoshiiy kleeyent nashiiy feermi. Ya yeevo kharasho znayu. Ocheen' preeyatniy cheelavyek. Oo meenya fstryechya s neem f cheetvyerk. Ocheen' vazhniee deela.

Tom *(On the phone...)* Alo, dobraye ootra, Barees Vadeemaveech. Gavareet Tom Walker... Da, spaseeba... da, kanyeshna vazmozhna... na slyedooshshyeeiy needyele... kanyeshna... da... ocheen' eenteeryesna... nyet, oo nas vryemya yes't'... preekrasna... nyet, tol'ka na nyeskal'ka dnyeiy... Ya paneemayu... kagda?... v voseem' cheesof... naveerkhoo, okala vikhada, okala dveeree. Noo, do ftorneeka, spaseeba balshoye, da sveedaneeya.

Kate Shto mi dyelaeem va ftorneek?

Tom Mi eedyom v reestaran s Bareesam Vadeemaveecheem. Reestaran f tsentree, za tserkav'yu. On gavareet, shto reestaran noviy. Barees Vadeemaveech v Maskvye na dva dnya, s Edith i Peeterom Palmer eez nashiiy feermi.

Kate Ya znayu Edith Palmer. Ana skoochnaya ee fsyo znayet loochshye vsyekh. Oo neeyo oozhasnaya sabaka. Ya doomayu, shto va ftorneek ya boodoo bal'na. Prastooda ee fsyo baleet. Vrachya nada boodeet vizvat'...

Tom Pazhalusta, tak neel'zya, tak nye gadeetsa. Barees Vadeemaveech ocheen' vazhniiy kleeyent.

47

(In the restaurant...)

Waiter Here's the menu. Today by us also firm's dishes (specials) – fish, and for sweet course – walnut cake.

Boris What for you, Mrs Walker? Soup you want? Meat or fish?

Kate For me steak with salad, please.

Edith To eat much red meat is harmful, Kate.

Boris Mr Walker, what for you? And what you want to drink? Wine?

Tom Beer, then sausage with fried potato, please.

Edith But Tom, that's very greasy! I would not want to eat such dishes.

Boris And you, Mrs Palmer?

Edith Small piece of chicken from grill, fruit and glass of water.

(Later...)

Boris Everyone ready? It is already late. Who wants coffee? No one? Good, bill, please.

Edith Oh, Boris Vadimovich, you can me help, please? How in Russian 'doggy bag'? I want bag for my dog.

Kate But Edith, your dog in England!

(In the restaurant...)

Waiter Vot meenyu. Seevodnya oo nas tozhe feermeeniee blyuda –
riba, ee na slatkaye – aryekhaviy tort.

Boris Shto vam, gaspazha Walker? Soop khateetee? Myasa eelee
riboo?

Kate Mnye beefshteks s salatam, pazhaloosta.

Edith Yes't' mnoga tyomnava myasa vryedna, Kate.

Boris Gaspadeen Walker, shto vam? Ee shto vi khateetye peet'?
Veeno?

Tom Peeva, patom kalbasoo z zhareenaiy kartoshkaiy, pazhaloosta.

Edith No Tom, eta ocheen' zhirna! Ya nye khatyela bi yes't' takoye
blyuda.

Boris A vi, gaspazha Palmer?

Edith Maleenkiy koosochyek kooreetsi, z greelya, frookti ee stakan
vadi.

(Later...)

Boris Fsye gatovi? Oozhe pozna. Kto khocheet kofee? Neekto?
Kharasho, shshyot, pazhaloosta.

Edith Akh, Barees Vadeemaveech, vi nee mozhitee mnye pamoch,
pazhaloosta? Kak pa-rooskee 'doggy bag'? Ya khachu
pakyeteek dlya mayeiy sabakee.

Kate No Edith, vasha sabaka v Anglee-ee!

New words

◀》 CD2, tr 6

kto-ta *someone*
pazvan**eet**'/pazvan**eel**
 to ring/he rang
on/yev**o**/neem *he, him*
skaz**at**'/skazal *to say/he said*
pachem**oo** *why*
n**o**meer *number*
boom**a**ga/boom**a**gee *paper*
okala *near, by*
kak**oiy**-ta *some (sort of)*
klee**ye**nt *customer*
kharash**o** *good, well*
f**ee**rma/f**ee**rmi *firm*
znat'/zn**a**yu/zn**a**eet *to know/*
 I know/he/(she) knows
cheelav**ye**k *person*
fstr**ye**chya *meeting*
cheetv**ye**rk *Thursday*
v**a**zhniee *important*
d**ye**la *matter*
gavar**eet**'/gavar**eet** *to speak,*
 to say/he speaks, he says
spas**ee**ba/balsh**oiy**e
 thank you/very much
kan**ye**shna *of course*
vazm**o**zhna *it is possible*
sl**ye**dooshshy**ee**iy *next*
eentee**rye**sna
 it is interesting
vr**ye**mya *time*
n**ye**skal'ka *a few*
dn**yeiy**/dn**ya** *days*
kagd**a** *when*

naveerkh**oo** *upstairs*
vikhad/vikh**a**da *exit*
dv**ye**r/dv**ee**ree *door*
ft**o**rneek/ft**o**rneeka *Tuesday*
ts**e**rkaf'/ts**e**rkav'yu *church*
oozh**a**snaya *terrible*
sab**a**ka *dog*
d**oo**mat'/d**oo**mayu
 to think/I think
b**oo**doo/b**oo**deet
 I will be/he (she, it) will be
bal'n**a** *ill, sick*
prast**oo**da *a cold*
bal**ee**t *it hurts*
vrach/vrach**ya** *doctor*
v**i**zvat'... *to summon,*
 call, send for
tak *thus, so*
nee gad**ee**tsa *it does not*
 fit (it's not on)
meen**yu** *menu*
f**ee**rmeeniee bl**yu**da
 firm's dishes (i.e. specials)
r**i**ba/ri**boo** *fish*
sl**a**tkaye *sweet, dessert*
ar**ye**khaviy tort *walnut cake*
gasp**a**zha *Mrs*
soop *soup*
m**ya**sa *meat*
beefsht**e**ks *steak*
sal**a**t/sal**a**tam *salad*
t**yo**mnava m**ya**sa *dark*
 (red) meat

vryedna *it is harmful*
gaspadeen *Mr*
veeno *wine*
peeva *beer*
kalbasa/kalbasoo *sausage*
zhareenaiy kartoshkaiy
  fried potato
zhirna *it is greasy*
koosocheek *piece*
kooreetsa/kooreetsi *chicken*

greel'/greelya *grill*
frookt *fruit*
stakan *glass*
vada/vadi *water*
gatovi *ready*
oozhe *already*
pozna *it is late*
neekto *no one*
pamoch' *to help*
kak pa-rooskee *how in Russian*

> **TOTAL NEW WORDS: 74**
> **...only 98 words to go!**

Last extras

Days of the week

paneedyel'neek	*Monday*	pyatneetsa	*Friday*
ftorneek	*Tuesday*	soobota	*Saturday*
sreeda	*Wednesday*	vaskreesyen'ye	*Sunday*
cheetvyerk	*Thursday*		

To say: *on Monday/Tuesday/Wednesday...,* etc. you add f (or va for *Tuesday*): f paneedyel'neek, va ftorneek, f sryedoo, f cheetvyerk, f pyatneetsoo, f soobotoo, v vaskreesyen'ye. Some of the endings change... Spot the differences!

Good news grammar

🔊 CD2, tr 7

1 Pronouns – useful!

These are worth learning because you'll need them all the time.

I = ya	*me* = meen**ya**	*to/for me* = mnye	*with me* = sa mnoiy
you = vi	*you* = vas	*to/for you* = vam	*with you* = s va**mee**
he = on	*him* = yeev**o**	*to/for him* = yem**oo**	*with him* = s neem
she = an**a**	*her* = yee**yo**	*to/for her* = yeiy	*with her* = s nyeiy
we = mi	*us* = nas	*to/for us* = nam	*with us* = s n**a**mee
they = an**ee**	*them* = eekh	*to for them* = eem	*with them* = s n**ee**mee

Learn one row at a time – down or across. Then put each word on a flash card and invest ten minutes a day. By the end of the week you'll know the lot!

2 The future – easy!

If you want to talk about something that is going to happen in the future, you could get away with using the present tense.

Mi **ye**deem f tsentr.	*We are going to the centre/We'll go to the centre.*
Seevodnya ya eed**oo** f reestar**an**.	*Today I am going (will go) to the restaurant.*

But if you want to say: *I'll, you'll,* or *he'll be…*, you say: ya b**oo**doo, on b**oo**deet, vi b**oo**deetye:

Va ftorneek ya b**oo**doo bal'n**a**.	*On Tuesday I will be ill.*

3 I would – would you?

To say *would* in Russian is fairly simple. Let's say: *I would buy…*

You take the past tense of *buy: bought* = koop**ee**la – and add the word bi:

Ya koop**ee**la bi…	*I would buy…*
An**a** khat**ye**la bi…	*She would like…*
Bar**ee**s skaz**al** bi…	*Boris would say...*

4 Short cut – leaving out the verb 'to go'

There's another bonus when using n**a**da, m**o**zhna or neelz'**ya**.

When you say that *it's necessary, possible or not possible to go somewhere* you can leave out the *go*: Nam nada v bank. *It's necessary for us (to go) to the bank.* Good shortcut!

5 Being polite

If you ask a question and want to be polite you use the negative. So, instead of asking: *Could you help me?*, you'll say *You could not help me, (by any chance, could you)?* i.e. Vi nee m**o**zhitee mnye pam**o**ch'?

Vi nee zn**a**eetee, gdye komnata 3?	*You don't know where room 3 is (by any chance, do you)?*

6 *Na, do, po, s, v, za:* lots for the price of a few!

These little words which tell you where things are (also known as prepositions) are most generous: each one has several meanings. Take n**a**. It can mean: *on, onto, to, at* and *for*. Here are some others:

do, da	*until, before, as far as*		s, z	*with, from*
po, pa	*along, on, according to*		v, f, va	*in, into, to, at*
za	*for, beyond, behind*			

Unfortunately, these prepositions do terrible things to the ending of the next word. But don't worry, you'll remember those when you learn your **Flash sentences** and **Learn by heart**.

Learn by heart

🔊 CD2, tr 8

This is a telephone call by a rather opinionated person… When you have learned it by heart try to act it out in less than a minute.

Vi khateetee eetee sa mnoiy v reestaran?

Ya znayu adeen ocheen' kharoshiiy reestaran.

Tam mozhna ocheen' vkoosna* payes't' ee veeno preekrasnaye.

Nyet, vi nee khateetye? Pacheemoo nyet? Ya ocheen' eenteeryesniiy cheelavyek!

Vi meenya nee znaeetee?

No kanyeshna, vi veedeetee** meenya po teeleeveezaroo.

Vi ne mozhitee? Pacheemoo nyet?

Oo vas vazhnaye fstryechya?

Eta neevazmozhna!

*fkoosna: *delicious* (the most commonly used word in Russian when praising food)

** veedeet'/veedeetee: *to see/you see*

Spot the keys

🔊 CD2, tr 9

This time you are in a department store and ask the sales assistant if the red T-shirt you fancy is also available in a size 40 (sarakavova razmyera).

You   Eezveeneeti, pazhaloosta, oo vas yes't' eta foodbolka sarakavova razmyera?

She says nyet, then **meenootachkoo, pazhaloosta** and goes into the stockroom. When she comes back, this is what she says:

Answer   *Noo, oonas takikh* foodbolok *astayotsaocheen'mala, oo nas seeychas* tol'ka zholtiee sarakavova razmyera. *Noo oonasyes't'yeeshshyo* krosniye foodbolkee treetsat' vas'mova razmyera. *Ee stil'takoiy, shtoyabiskazala, shto* treetsat' vas'moiy razmyer vam gadeetsa.

Did you get the key words? Size 40 was only available in yellow. They have red in 38, which should fit.

Say it simply

When people want to speak Russian but don't dare, it's usually because they are trying to translate what they want to say from English into Russian. And when they don't know some of the words, they give up!

With **Fast Russian with Elisabeth Smith** you work around the words you don't know with the words you do know! Believe me, with some 400 words you can say anything! It may not always be very elegant, but you are communicating!

Here are two examples showing you how to say things in a simple way. Words that are not part of the vocabulary are in **bold**.

1 You need to **change** your **flight** from Tuesday to Friday.

Mi nye mozhim **ye**khat' va ftorneek. Mi khat**ee**m samal**yo**t
f p**ya**tneetsoo.
We cannot travel on Tuesday. We want (an) aeroplane on Friday.

or

Ftorneek nam nee gad**ee**tsa. Mi khat**ee**m **ye**khat' f p**ya**tneetsoo.
Tuesday does not fit (suit). We want to travel on Friday.

2 Your **watch** is **broken** and you need to have it mended before you leave.

Eezveen**ee**tee, pazhaloosta, n**a**da atr**ee**manteeravat' chees**i**,
an**ee** nee rab**o**tayut. Z'dyes' yes't' magaz**ee**n, gdye m**o**zhna
skar**ye**ye atr**ee**manteeravat' eekh?

Excuse me please, it is necessary to repair clock not working. Here is there shop where possible in a hurry repair them?

Let's speak Russian

🔊 CD2, tr 9

Here are ten sentences to warm-up, and then on to greater things.

1 Who has said that?
2 I don't know why.
3 You to help? (can I help you?)
4 We have time – on Monday, I believe.
5 I want to drive to Moscow.
6 He would like to know that.
7 Work on Sunday? That's not on!
8 Do you want my number?
9 Chicken for me, please.
10 Yes, of course, I have an appointment.

Now pretend you are in Russia with friends who do not speak Russian. They will want you to ask people things in Russian, such as *Please ask him...*

11 if he knows Edith Palmer.
12 if he is going to the restaurant with us on Tuesday.
13 if she would like meat or fish and fried potato.
14 if they have an appointment today.
15 if they know where the restaurant is.

Now your friends ask you to tell people things. This time there may be words you don't know, so you have to work round it using words you do. They say: *Please tell her...*

16 that the soup is very delicious.
17 that unfortunately the shower is not in working order.
18 that we would like a meal with them.
19 that you are allergic to fish.
20 that Saturday will suit us.

Answers

1 Kto skazal **e**ta?
2 Ya ne zn**a**yu, pacheem**oo**.
3 Vam pam**o**ch'?
4 Oo nas vryem**ya** yes't' – f paneed**ye**l'neek, k**a**zhitsa.
5 Ya khachu **ye**khat' v Maskv**oo**.
6 On khat**ye**l bi znat' **e**ta.
7 Rab**o**tat' v vaskrees**ye**n'ye? Tak nye gad**ee**tsa!
8 Vi khat**ee**tee moiy n**o**meer?
9 Mnye k**oo**reets**oo**, pazhal**oo**sta.
10 Da, kany**e**shna, oo meen**ya** fstry**e**chya.
11 Vi zn**a**eetee Edith Palmer?
12 Vi eed**yo**tee s n**a**mee v reestar**a**n va ft**o**rneek?
13 Vi khat**ee**tee m**ya**sa **ee**lee r**i**boo z zhar**e**enaiy kart**o**shkaiy?
14 Yes't' oo vas fstry**e**chya seev**o**dnya.
15 Vi nee zn**a**eetee, gdye reestar**a**n?
16 Soop **o**cheen' fk**oo**sniy.
17 K sazhil**ye**neeyu doosh nye rab**o**taeet.
18 M**o**zhna eet**ee** v reestar**a**n?
19 On/ana nee yes't' r**i**boo.
20 Soob**o**ta nam gad**ee**tsa.

Let's speak more Russian

🔊 CD2, tr 11

For these optional exercises add an extra 15 minutes to your daily schedule. And remember: near enough is good enough!

In your own words

This exercise will teach you to express yourself freely. Use only the words you have learned so far.

Tell me in your own words that...

1 Mr Ivanov rang you
2 he is a good client of your firm
3 you are going to a restaurant with him on Saturday evening
4 it is possible to meet next week
5 Kate can't go, she has important business
6 Tom has a cold, we must call a doctor
7 you will take steak, fish with potato, a small piece of chicken and salad, tea and cake, please

Ask:

8 Do you have any specials today?
9 Have you known him long?
10 What do you want to drink?

Answers

1 Mnye pazvaneel gaspadeen Eevanof.
2 On kharoshiiy kleeyent nashiiy feermi.
3 F soobotoo vyecheeram mi s neem eedyom v reestaran.
4 Vazmozhno vstryeteetsa na slyedooshshyeeiy needyelee.
5 Kate nye mozhit eetee, oo neeyo vazhnaie deela.
6 Oo Toma prastooda, nada vizvat' vrachya.
7 Mnye, pazhaloosta beefshteks/riboo s kartoshkaiy/koosocheek kooritsi ee salat/chyaiy ee tort.
8 Oo vas yes't' seevodnya feermeeniee blyuda?
9 Vi yeevo davno znaeetee?
10 Shto vi khateetee peet'?

Let's speak Russian – fast and fluently

🔊 CD2, tr 12

Translate each section and check if it is correct. Then cover the answers and say the three or four sentences fast!

Can you say each section in 25 seconds?
Some of the English is in 'Russian-speak' to help you.

Today called Boris.
He is our client, very good man.
He in Moscow for two days. By his important meeting.

Seevodnya pazvaneel Barees.
On nash kleeyent, ocheen' kharoshiiy cheelavyek.
On v Maskvye na dva dnya. Oo neevo vazhnaye fstryechya.

What shall we do tomorrow?
In centre, behind church is new restaurant.
By you have time?

Shto mi dyelaeem zaftra?
F tsentree, za tserkvayu yes't' noviy reestaran.
Oo vas yes't' vryemya?

I can't. By me ill wife, necessary it will be to call doctor.
I understand, it's a pity, but on next week?

Ya nee magoo. Oo meenya bal'na zhina, nada boodeet vizvat' vrachya.
Ya panimayu, ocheen' zhal', a na slyedooshsheeiy needyelee?

Now say all the sentences in Russian without stopping and starting.
If you are not happy with your result – just try once more!

Test your progress

Translate the following sentences in writing. Then check the answers.

1 I think the appointment is on Tuesday.
2 Today? No, I am sorry, that is not possible.
3 I must buy many presents.
4 Can('t) you help me, please? I want the number of the doctor.
5 Do(n't) you know where there is a good restaurant?
6 The church is very interesting, it seems.
7 We would like to travel on Monday evening, please.
8 Can I have the menu, please?
9 Excuse me, please, where are the papers?
10 Can one buy fruit here?
11 Do you know his new restaurant?
12 It was wonderful! Thank you very much for the pleasant evening.
13 Why is it necessary for you to see my credit card?
14 It was boring at the theatre on Monday.
15 You see the telephone upstairs by the exit, by the door.
16 We eat chicken or sausage... the fish is too expensive.
17 How does one say in Russian...?
18 Do(n't) you know where here bus? (where there is a bus here?)
19 My husband wants to go to Texas, but I would like to go to New York.
20 He does not know that the new restaurant is behind the church.

How did you get on? Another brilliant score on the **Progress chart**?

Week 5

Day-by-day guide

How about 15 minutes on the train, tube or bus, 10 minutes on the way home and 30 minutes before switching on the television…?

Day one
- Read **On their way**.
- Listen to/Read **F pootee**.
- Read the **New words**. Learn 15 or more.

Day two
- Repeat the dialogue. Learn the harder **New words**
- Cut out the **Flash words** to get stuck in.

Day three
- Test yourself to perfection on all the **New words**.
- Read and learn the **Good news grammar**.

Day four (the tough day)
- Listen to/Read **Learn by heart**.
- Cut out and learn the ten **Flash sentences**.

Day five
- Listen to/Read **Spot the keys**.
- Go over **Learn by heart**.

Day six
- Listen to/Read **Let's speak Russian**.
- Listen to/Read **Let's speak more Russian** (optional).
- Listen to/Read **Let's speak Russian – fast and fluently** (optional).
- Translate **Test your progress**.

Day seven
I bet you don't want a day off… but I insist!

On their way

Tom and Kate travel across Russia by train, bus and taxi.

(At the station...)

Tom Two tickets to Tver, please.

Clerk There and back?

Tom There and how (what)? More slowly, please.

Clerk There... and... back.

Tom To one end (single) only, please. When leaves train and from where?

Clerk At 9.45, from fifth platform.

Kate More quickly (hurry), Tom, here are two places, for non-smokers. Oh, here is someone here smoking. Excuse me, in the train not possible to smoke. Because these seats are for non-smokers. Here to smoke is forbidden.

Man Sorry, I don't understand. I speak only English.

(At the bus stop...)

Kate On Sundays few buses. For us it is necessary to wait 20 minutes. Tom, here are my postcards and letter. Over there post box. And I want to take couple of photographs. River so beautiful in sun.

Tom Kate, hurry. Are arriving two buses. Both yellow. First already full, the other is better.

(In the bus...)

Driver Tickets it is necessary to punch!

Tom Oh, yes, thank you. To museum it is far?

Driver This bus goes not to museum, but to hospital.

F pootee

🔊 CD2, tr 13

Tom and Kate travel across Russia by train, bus and taxi.

(Na vagzalee...)

Tom   Dva beelyeta f Tvyer, pazhaloosta.

Clerk   Tooda ee abratna?

Tom   Tooda ee kak? Pamyedleeneeye, pazhaloosta.

Clerk   Tooda... ee... abratna.

Tom   Tol'ka, v adeen kanyets pazhaloosta. Kagda atkhodeet poeest ee atkooda?

Clerk   V dyeveet' sorak pyat', ot pyataiy platformi.

Kate   Skaryeye, Tom, vot dva myesta, dlya neekooryashsheekh. Akh, vot kto-ta z'dyes' kooreet'. Eezveeneetee, f poeezdee neel'zya kooreet'. Patamoo shta etee meesta dlya neekooryashsheekh. Z'dyes' kooreet' zapreeshaeetsa.

Man   Sorry, I don't understand. Ya gavaryu only English.

(Na astanofkee aftoboosa...)

Kate   Pa vaskreesyen'yam mala aftoboosaf. Nam nada zhdat' dvatsat meenoot. Tom, vot maee atrkitkee ee pees'mo. Von tam pachtoviy yashsheek. A ya khachoo s'nyat' paroo fatagrafeeiy. Reeka tak kraseeva na sontsi.

Tom   Kate, skaryeye! Vot dva aftoboosa. Oba zholtiee. Pyervyiy oozhe polan, droogoiy loochshi.

(F avtoboosee...)

Driver   Beelyeti nada prakampas'teeravat'!

Tom   Akh, da, kanyeshna. Do moozyeya daleeko?

Driver   Etat aftoboos yedeet nye v moozyeiy, a v bal'neetsoo.

(In the taxi...)

Tom   I very pleased. Taxi not bad and journey not too expensive costs.

Kate   To me does not please this car (I don't like), because it old and not clean... that's why cheaper. I hope that problems will not be.

Tom   There was only this taxi. *(Later...)* Where we? I don't see museum. On left petrol station and station of metro. On right school.

Kate   Here is plan of town. To museum, it seems, it is not far... to traffic lights, then right along main street. Why we so slowly travelling? Petrol has finished? Oil has finished? Taxi has broken down? Where my bag? Where mobile phone?

Tom   Kate, these questions lead me from mind (are driving me crazy). And it is raining. And why police travelling behind us?

(F taksee...)

Tom   Ya **o**cheen' dav**o**leen. Taks**ee** neeplakh**o**ye ee pa**ye**stka nye sl**ee**shkam d**o**raga st**o**eet.

Kate   Mnye nye nr**a**veetsa **e**ta mash**i**na, patam**oo** shta st**a**raya ee nyech**ee**staya, vot pacheem**oo** deesh**e**vlee. Ya nad**ye**yus', shto prabl**ye**m nye b**oo**deet.

Tom   B**i**la t**o**l'ka **e**ta taks**ee**. *(Pozhe...)* Gdye mi? Ya nee v**ee**zhoo mooz**ye**iy. Nal**ye**va benzazapr**a**fka ee st**a**ntseeya m**ee**tr**o**. Napr**a**va shk**o**la.

Kate   Vot plan g**o**rada. Da mooz**ye**ya, k**a**zhitsa, needaleek**o**... da sveetaf**o**ra, pat**o**m napr**a**va po gl**a**vnaiy **oo**leetsi. Pacheem**oo** mi tak m**ye**dleena **ye**deem? Beenz**ee**n k**o**ncheels'a? M**a**sla k**o**ncheelas'? Taks**ee** slam**a**las? Gdye m**a**ya s**oo**mka? Gdye s**o**taviy teel**ee**f**o**n?

Tom   Kate, **e**tee vapr**o**see sv**o**dyat meen**ya** s **oo**ma. Ee eed**yo**t dosht'. A pacheem**oo** meel**ee**tsiya **ye**deet za nam**ee**?

New words

◀ CD2, tr 14

poot'/pootee *way, journey*
vagzal *(railway) station*
beelyet/beelyety *ticket/tickets*
dva beelyeta *two tickets*
tooda *to there*
abratna *back/return*
pamyedleeneeye *a little more slowly*
kanyets *end, direction (one way)*
atkhadeet'/atkhodeet *to leave/it leaves*
poeest/f poeezdee *train/in the train*
atkooda *from where*
platforma/platformi *platform*
skaryeye *hurry*
neekooryashsheekh *non-smokers*
kooreet' *to smoke*
patamoo shta *because*
zapreeshshaeetsa *it is forbidden*
astanofka *bus stop*
pa vaskreesyeneeyam *on Sundays*
mala *few, little*
zhdat' *to wait*
pees'mo *letter*
von tam *over there*
pachtoviy yashsheek *post box*
snyat' *to take (of photographs)*
para/paroo *pair, couple*
fatagrafiya/fatagrafeeiy *photograph/photographs*
reeka *river*
sontse *sun*
oba *both*

pyervyiy *first*
polan *full*
droogoiy *other, another*
prakampasteeravat' *to punch, clip*
moozyeiy/moozyeya *museum*
(nee) daleeko *it is (not) far, (not) distant*
etat/eta *this*
bal'neetsa/bal'neetsoo *hospital*
neeplakhoye *not bad*
payestka *journey*
mashina *car*
staroye/staraya *old*
neecheestaya *not clean*
nadyeyatsa/nadyeyus' *to hope/I hope*
taksee *taxi*
eedyot dosht' *it's raining*
veedeet'/veezhoo *to see/I see*
beenzazaprafka *petrol station (colloquial)*
stantseeya meetro *metro station*
shkola *school*
plan gorada *plan of the town*
sveetafor/sveetafora *traffic lights*
glavnaiy ooleetsi *main street*
myedleena *slowly*
beenzeen *petrol*
koncheelsa/koncheelas' *has finished*
masla *oil*
slamalas' *it has broken down*
svodyat meenya s ooma *are driving me crazy*
meeleetsiya *police*

> **TOTAL NEW WORDS: 60**
> ...only 38 words to go!

68

Learn by heart

🔊 CD2, tr 15

Someone crashed the car and someone else is getting suspicious!

> ## Mashina tol'ka neemnoshka slamalas...
>
> **Za**ftra nam mozhna smat**ryet' te**nees? Oo meen**ya** dva beel**ye**ta
> na mach. Ya khach**u vee**deet' n**o**vykh ameereek**a**nskeekh tinees**ee**staf.*
> M**o**zhna **ye**khat' t**oo**da na meetr**o**? **Ee**lee l**oo**chshe na aft**o**boosee,
> patam**oo** shta on **ye**deet pr**ya**ma na stadee**o**n.
> Aft**o**boos? Meetr**o**? Pacheem**oo**? Mnye nye nr**a**veetsa garatsk**oiy**
> transp**a**rt. Oo nas kras**ee**vaya mash**i**na.
> Da, no... vcheer**a**, kagd**a** ya **ye**khala v g**o**rat, ya nee oov**ee**deela
> sveetaf**o**r... no mash**i**na t**o**l'ka nyemn**o**shka slam**a**las...
>
> *tinees**ee**staf: *tennis players*

Good news grammar

◀)) CD2, tr 16

1 *nraveetsa* – to like – or not like

Think how often you use this in English: *I like this – you don't like that – do you like…?* In Russian you use n**ra**veetsa, but it is a bit of a strange construction. Think of it as *something that is pleasing to you*:

I like the car –	Mnye nr**a**veetsa mash**i**na.
To me is pleasing the car.	
We don't like the car –	Nam nye nr**a**veetsa mash**i**na.
To us is not pleasing the car.	
Do you like to work? –	Vam nr**a**veetsa rabot**at**'?
To you is pleasing to work?	

Once you get used to *is pleasing* it's quite simple really. Just remember nr**a**veetsa.

2 Saying the opposite – just add *nee*

This an easy way to double your vocabulary! As opposed to learning two words just use one and add n**ee**:

Eta kras**ee**viy g**o**rat.	*It is a beautiful town.*
Eta n**ee**kras**ee**viy g**o**rat.	*It is an ugly (not beautiful) town.*
Magz**ee**nee neeinter**ye**snyee.	*The shops are boring (not interesting).*

3 Another shortcut – 'can' and 'can't'

In such common phrases as *Can you hear…?* or *Can't you see…?* the Russians will leave out the *can* or *can't* altogether:

Ya sl**i**shoo yeev**o**.	*I can hear him.*
Vi nye v**ee**deetee teeleev**ee**zar?	*Can't you see the television?*

Let's speak Russian

◀) CD2, tr 17

A ten-point warm-up: I give you an answer and you ask me a question as if you did not hear the words in CAPITAL LETTERS very well.

Example: Veektar Z'DYES'. *Question* Gdye Veektar?

1 Sotaviy teeleefon V SOOMKEE.
2 SHKOLA von tam.
3 Poeest atkhodeet V TREE CHEESA.
4 TOM khocheet gavareet' s Bareesam Eevanaveecheem.
5 Beelyet tooda ee abratna stoeet 80 ROOBLYEIY.
6 Mnye nye nraveetsa mashina, PATAMOO SHTA ana staraya.
7 Vi yedeetee v Angleeyu … NA SAMALYOTEE.
8 Ya oveedeel(a) SVEETAFOR.
9 DA, mnye nraveetsa gasteeneetsa.
10 Mnye nraveetsa MOOZYEIY.

Now answer starting with 'da':

11 Vi znaeetee noviy magazeen?
12 Vam nraveetsa reeka?
13 Vi veedeetee astanofkoo aftoboosa?

Here are three things that you want to refer to. But you don't know what they are called in Russian. Explain them using the words you know:

14 a refrigerator
15 a holiday
16 a kennel

Answers

1 Gdye sotavyiy teeleefon?
2 Shto eta von tam?
3 Kagda atkhodeet poeest?
4 Kto khocheet gavereet' s Bareesam Eevanaveecheem?
5 Skol'ka stoeet beelyet tooda ee abratna?
6 Pacheemoo vam nye nraveetsa mashina?
7 Kak vi yedeete v Angleeyu?
8 Shto vi ooveedeelee?
9 Vam nraveetsa gasteeneetsa?
10 Shto vam nraveetsa?
11 Da, ya znayu noviy magazeen.
12 Da, mnye nraveetsa reeka.
13 Da, ya veezhoo astanofkoo aftoboosa.
14 Meesta, gdye kholadna, dlya malaka, myasa, sira.
15 Vryemya, kagda vi nye rabotaeetee.
16 Dom dlya sabakee, kagda mi v otpooskee.

Let's speak more Russian

🔊 CD2, tr 18

In your own words

This exercise will teach you to express yourself freely. Use only the words you have learned so far.

Tell me in your own words that...

1 the train leaves at 10.30 from the first platform
2 you hope there won't be any problems
3 on Saturdays there are few buses; it is necessary to wait for a long time
4 it is necessary to punch the tickets
5 the taxi is not expensive, but the car is old
6 you need two tickets to St Petersburg, there and back
7 you want to take a couple of photos, the church is so beautiful
8 you are driving along the main street to the railway station, then to the right
9 you can't see the taxi

Ask:

10 where are seats for non-smokers?

Answers

1 Poeesd atkhodeet v dyeseet' treetsat ot pyervaiy platformi.
2 Ya nadyeyus', shto prablyem nye boodeet.
3 Pa soobotam mala aftoboosaf, nada dolgo zhdat'.
4 Nada prakampasteeravat' beelyety.
5 Taksee stoeet nyedoraga, no mashina staraya.
6 Mnye dva beelyeta f Sankt-Peeteerboork, tooda i abratna.
7 Ya khachu snyat' paroo fatagrafeeiy, tserkaf tak kraseevaya.
8 Mi yedeem po glavnaiy ooleetsi do vagzala, patom naprava.
9 Ya nee veezhoo taksee.
10 Gdye meesta dlya neekooryashsheekh?

73

Let's speak Russian – fast and fluently

◀》 CD2, tr 19

Translate each section and check if it is correct. Then cover the answers and say the three or four sentences as quickly as you can. Try to say each section in less than 30 seconds.

Ticket one way to Tver. How much?
More slowly, please. Yes, for me on train at 11.30.
Where platform number 5?

Beel**yet** v ad**ee**n kan**ye**ts f Tv**ye**r'. Sk**o**l'ka?
Pam**ye**dleeneeye, pazhal**oo**sta. Da, mnye na p**o**eest v adinatsat tritsat.
Gdye platf**o**rma n**o**meer pyat?

We need the post box.
Here are letter and photo.
More quickly, the bus is full again.
Other one it necessary to wait ten minutes.

Nam n**oo**zhin pacht**o**viy **ya**shsheek.
Vot pees'm**o** ee fatagr**a**fiya.
Skar**ye**ye, aft**o**boos apyat' p**o**lan.
Droog**o**iy n**a**da zhdat' d**ye**seet' meen**oo**t.

Ten minutes wait, let's go on taxi.
To the metro, it seems, not far.
Along the main street, to the traffic light, then to the left.
Where my mobile phone?

D**ye**seet' min**oo**t zhdat', **ye**deem na taks**ee**.
Do m**ee**tro, k**a**zhitsa, nyedal**ee**ko.
Po gl**a**vnaiy **oo**leetsi, do sveetaf**o**ra, patom nal**ye**va.
Gdye moiy s**o**taviy teel**ee**fon?

Spot the keys

🔊 CD2, tr 20

This time you are planning a trip in the country and want to have some idea what the weather will be like. This is what you could ask:

You   Eezveeneetee, pazhaloosta, vi nye mozhitee mnye skazat', kakaya zaftra boodeet pagoda?

Answer   *Eezveeneetee, ya nee znayu, no kagdayasmatryel* pragnoz pagodi po teeleeveezaroo, *skazalee, shto pagoda* myedleena *meenyaeetsa.* Zaftra *boodeet kholadna* – voseem' gradoosaf, s *neebal'shimvyetram ee* dosht boodeet k vyecheeroo.

She doesn't know, but according to the TV something slow is happening and it will be cold tomorrow, 8°C, with rain in the evening.

Test your progress

1 I don't like this bag. The other bag was better.

2 How much does (the) ticket cost – return?

3 What did you say? Slowly, please.

4 I know that in America petrol is cheaper.

5 In (the) underground it is forbidden to smoke.

6 I cannot wait, I have (an) appointment at 11 o'clock.

7 Is this (the) letter box? (A) yellow letter box?

8 Hello, we are 30 km from Novgorod. Is that (the) petrol station?

9 Which is cheaper? (The) bus or (the) metro?

10 Today it is very cold. I hope that it will rain.

11 The traffic light was red, not green. That's why they're both in hospital.

12 She was at (the) petrol station on Monday and Tuesday. The car drinks petrol!

13 Where here (is the) dry cleaner's? By me oil on T-shirt 'Armani'.

14 Our flat (is) behind (the) main street, by (the) bus stop.

15 We are by police (at the police station), because we do not know where my mobile phone (is).

16 It is necessary to buy (the) tickets now, because they cheaper.

17 I like your car. Was it very expensive?

18 Can you help us, please? Can one eat here by river?

If you know all your words you should score over 90%!

Week 6
Day-by-day guide

This is your last week! Need I say more?

Day one
- Read **In the airport**.
- Listen to/Read **V aerapartoo**.
- Read the **New words**. There are only a handful!

Day two
- Read **V aerapartoo**. Learn all the **New words**.
- Work with the **Flash words** and **Flash sentences**.

Day three
- Test yourself on the **Flash sentences**.
- No more **Good news grammar**! Try the quiz instead.

Day four
- Listen to/Read and learn **Da sveedaneeya**.
- Listen to/Read **Spot the keys**.

Day five
- Listen to/Read **Let's speak Russian**.
- Read **Say it simply**.

Day six
- Listen to/Read **Let's speak more Russian** (optional).
- Listen to/Read **Let's speak Russian – fast and fluently** (optional).
- Your last **Test your progress**! Go for it!

Day seven

> **Congratulations!**
> **You have successfully completed the course**
> **and can now speak**
> ***Fast Russian with Elisabeth Smith!***

In the airport

Tom and Kate are on their way back to Birmingham. They are in the departure lounge at Moscow airport.

Tom On Monday for us it is necessary will be to work. Terrible! I want (to go) to Italy or to Hawaii! No one in my firm nows where I (am).

Kate And in my firm? They know (the) number of telephone of my mother, and she knows the number of my mobile telephone...

Tom Yes, yes, I know. Well, perhaps at Christmas, (a) week in the snow or let's go on (a) ship to Madeira. But I want to buy (a) newspaper downstairs... Kate! There is Yuriy Zhivago!

Yuriy Hello! How are things? What you here are doing? This is my wife, Nancy. Already (the) end of your holiday? Well, how all went? (How did it go?)

Kate Splendidly! (wonderful). We much saw and too much ate. Now we well know Moscow, and Saint Petersburg...

Yuriy Next year for you it is necessary to (go to) Novgorod! Mrs Walker, my wife wants to buy a book for our computer. You (not) can help her (Could you help her at all?) Mr Walker, you have a newspaper. Give, please, (the) Sport. Then I invite you to (the) bar.

(At the airport kiosk...)

Kate Here nothing suitable there is [not]. You also going to England?

Nancy No, we are going to Saint Petersburg. Mother of Yuriy lives there. Our children were by her for two weeks. By us (we have) boy and three girls. Tomorrow we are going to Novgorod on the train. It is cheaper.

Kate Your husband works in (a) bank?

Nancy Yes, his work (is) interesting, but money (is) not big. To our Lada already nine years (our Lada is already nine years old) and by us (we have) old, small flat. (In) this year much (we) have repaired. My parents and my girlfriend (are) in (the) USA and we often write letters. I would like (to go) to America, but too expensive costs.

78 Kate But by you (you have) (a) beautiful house in Greece.

V aerapartoo

🔊 CD2, tr 21

Tom and Kate are on their way back to Birmingham. They are in the departure lounge of Moscow airport.

Tom F paneed**ye**lneek n**a**m nada b**oo**deet rabotat'. **Oo**zhas! Ya khach**u** v It**a**leeyu **ee**lee na Gav**ai**yee! Neek**to** v ma**yeiy** f**ee**rmee nye zn**a**eet, gdye ya.

Kate A v ma**yeiy** f**ee**rmee? An**ee** zn**a**yut n**o**meer teel**ee**fona ma**yeiy** m**a**mi, a an**a** zn**a**eet n**o**meer mayev**o** s**o**tavava teel**ee**fona.

Tom Da, da, zn**a**yu. Noo, m**o**zhit bit' na Razhd**ee**stv**o**, need**ye**lyu f snyeg**oo ee**lee pay**e**deem na teeplakh**o**dee na Mad**yeiy**roo. A ya khach**u** koop**ee**t' gaz**ye**too vnee**zoo**... Kate! Vot **Yu**riy Zhiv**a**ga!

Yuriy Zdr**a**stvooiytee! Kak d**ee**l**a**? Shto vi z'dyes' d**ye**la**ee**tee? **E**ta m**aya** zhin**a**, Nancy. **Oo**zh**e** kan**ye**ts v**a**shiva **o**tp**oo**ska? Noo, kak fsyo prashl**o**?

Kate Veeleekal**ye**pna! Mi mn**o**ga v**ee**deelee ee sl**ee**shkam mn**o**ga **ye**lee. Seechy**a**s mi kharash**o** zn**a**eem ee Maskv**oo** ee Sankt-Peeteerb**oo**rk...

Yuriy F sl**ye**dooshsheem gad**oo** vam n**a**da v N**o**vgarat! Gaspazh**a** Walker, m**aya** zhin**a** kh**o**cheet koop**ee**t' kn**ee**goo dlya n**a**shiva kamp**'yu**tira. Vi nye m**o**zhitee yeiy pam**o**ch'? Gaspad**ee**n Walker, oo vas gaz**ye**ta. D**ai**ytee, pazh**a**loosta, *Sport*. Pat**o**m preeglash**a**yu vas v bar.

*(V aerapart**oo**, ookee**oo**ska...)*

Kate Z'dyes' neech**ee**vo patkhad**ya**shsheeva nyet. Vi t**o**zhe **ye**deetee v **A**ngleeyu?

Nancy Nyet, mi **ye**deem f Sankt-Peeteerb**oo**rk. M**a**ma **Yu**riiya zhiv**yo**t tam. N**a**shi d**ye**tee b**i**lee oo ne**e**yo dvye need**ye**lee. Oo nas mal'ch**ee**k ee tree d**ye**vachkee. Z**a**ftra mi **ye**deem v N**o**vgarat na p**o**eezdee. **E**ta deesh**e**vlee.

Kate Vash moosh rab**o**taeet v b**a**nkee?

Nancy Da, yeev**o** rab**o**ta eenteer**ye**snaya, no d**ye**n'gee nyebal'sh**i**ee. Nash**ee**iy L**a**dee **oo**zh**e** d**ye**veet' lyet ee oo nas star**a**ya, m**a**leen'kaya kvart**ee**ra. V et**a**m gad**oo** mn**o**ga atreem**a**nt**ee**ravalee. M**a**ee rad**ee**teelee ee padr**oo**ga f S-SHA ee mi ch**ya**sta p**ee**shim p**ee**s'ma. Ya **o**cheen' khat**ye**la bi v Am**ye**reek**oo**, no sl**ee**shkam d**o**raga st**o**eet.

Kate No oo vas kras**ee**vyiy dom v Gr**ye**tsi-ee.

79

Nancy (A) house in Greece? I never [not] was in Greece (I have never been to Greece). When by us (we have) (a) holiday, we go to friend('s), at Cheel**ya**beensk.

Tom Kate, hurry, for us it is time (to go). What said Mrs Zhivago?

Kate Wait, Tom, wait!

New words

🔊 CD2, tr 22

Ital**ee**ya/It**al**eeyu *Italy/to Italy*
Gav**aiy**ee *Hawaii*
m**a**mi/m**a**ma *mother*
Razhd**ee**stvo *Christmas*
snyek/sneeg**oo** *snow*
pa**ye**deem *let's go*
teeplakh**ot**/teeplakh**o**dee *ship*
Mad**yeiy**ra/Mad**yeiy**roo *Madeira*
vnee**zoo** *downstairs*
kak deel**a**? *how are things?*
prashl**o** *it went by, passed*
veeleekal**ye**pna *splendid(ly),
    great, wonderful(ly)*
yelee *we/they ate*
fs**lye**doosshshee/**e**tam gadoo
    next/this year
kn**ee**ga *book*
d**aiy**tee *give!*
preeglash**at**'/preeglash**a**yu
    to invite/I invite
bar *bar*
neech**ee**vo *nothing*

patkhad**ya**shsheeiy/
    patkhad**ya**shsheeva *suitable*
zhivy**ot** *lives*
d**ye**tee *children*
dvye(f) *two*
mal'cheek *boy*
d**ye**vachka/d**ye**vachkee *(little)
    girl/girls*
deesh**ye**vlee *cheaper*
moosh *husband*
Lada/Ladoo *Lada*
lyet *of years*
maleen'keeiy/m**a**leen'kaya
    small
S-SHA *USA*
p**ee**shim *we write*
ch**ya**sta *often*
p**ee**s'ma *letters*
neekagd**a** nee *never*
droog/dr**oo**goo *friend*
par**a** *it is time (to go)*
padazhd**ee**! *wait!*

> **TOTAL NEW WORDS: 38**
> **Total Russian words learned: 381**
> **Extra words: 80**
> **GRAND TOTAL: 461**

Nancy	Dom v Gryetsi-ee? Ya neekagda nee bila v Gryetsi-ee. Kagda oo nas otpoosk, mi yedeem k droogoo f Cheelyabeensk.
Tom	Kate! Skaryeye, nam para! Shto skazala gaspazha Zhivaga?
Kate	Padazhdee, Tom, padazhdee!

Learn by heart

◀) CD2, tr 23

This is your last dialogue to **Learn by heart**. Give it your best!
You now have six prize-winning party pieces, and a large store
of everyday sayings which will be very useful.

Da sveedaneeya!

Kate   Barees Vadeemaveech, gavareet Kate Walker, a ya
v aerapartoo v Maskvye. Da, oozhe kanyets nashiva
otpooska ee nasheekh dyeneek tozhe! Spaseeba
balshoye za ocheen' preeyatniiy vyecheer! Tom
khocheet gavareet' s vamee.

Tom   Zdrastvooiytee, Barees Vadeemaveech... Kak? Vi
khateetee koopeet'oba? Oo mayeiy feermi yes't'
vash e-mail? Veeleekalyepna. Spaseeba balshoye!
F slyedooshsheem gadoo?... Kate khocheet v Italeeyu,
no mnye nraveetsa Raseeya.* S Edith Palmer? Akh, Bozhe
moiy, nyet, nyet! Nash samalyot zhdyot**... Noo... Da
sveedaneeya!

*Raseeya: *Russia*
**zhdyot: *is waiting*

Good news grammar

There's no more grammar this week, just a couple of interesting points.

1 Double negative

The Russians love to say nyet so they sometimes say it twice!

Neekto nye znaeet, gdye ya.   *No one not knows where I am.*
Ya neekagda nye bila v Gryetsi-ee.   *I never not was in Greece.*

2 Surnames

Yuriy Baranav… and his wife, Mrs Baranava. In Russian, a man's surname usually ends in a consonant and a woman's in the letter 'a' (thus Anna Karyeneena's husband's surname was Karyeneen).

3 Quiz

And now for some light relief: the end of course quiz!

No marks for this one – just a pat on the back!

1 In which city would you find the *Kryeml'*?
   a Sankt-Peeteerboork   c Yalta
   b Maskva   d Vladeevastok

2 How would you say 12 o'clock in Russian?
   a dva cheesa   c dveenatsat' cheesof
   b dvatsat' cheesof

3 How would you greet someone if you met them in the evening?
   a dobraye ootra   c da sveedaneeya
   b dobriiy dyen'   d dobriiy vyecheer

4 If you were a vegetarian, which of these would you not eat?
   a myasa   c tort
   b frookti   d kartoshka

5 When do you celebrate Christmas in Russia?

    a 24 deekabr**ya**   **c** 31 deekabr**ya**

    b 25 deekabr**ya**   **d** 6 yeenvar**ya**

6 If you wanted to apologize, what would you say?

    a kharasho   **c** oozh**a**sna

    b eezveen**ee**tee   **d** kan**ye**shna

7 When does *Dyet Maros* (the Russian version of Father Christmas) bring presents?

    a 24 deekabr**ya**   **c** 31 deekabr**ya**

    b 25 deekabr**ya**   **d** 6 yeenvar**ya**

8 What does *shto vam* mean?

    a Where are you?   **c** Where do you work?

    b What would you like?

9 How do you say in Russian *I understand*?

    a ya paneem**a**yu   **c** ya khach**u**

    b ya zn**a**yu   **d** ya mag**oo**

10 What do Russians say when they really don't approve of what you want to do?

    a tak m**o**zhna   **c** tak n**a**da

    b tak neel'**zya**   **d** tak nye gad**ee**tsa

You'll find the answers in the **Answers** section.

Spot the keys

🔊 CD2, tr 24

Here's a final practice round. If you have the recording, close the book now. Find the key words and try to get the gist of it. Then check your answers.

This is what you might ask a taxi driver:

You	Skol'k**a** meen**oo**t do aerap**o**rta ee sk**o**l'ka st**o**eet?
Answer	*Eta zaveeseet ot tavo, kagda vi yedeetee. Abichna payestka dleetsa dvatsat' meenoot, no yeslee vi khateetee yekhat' f chyasee peek ee veez'dee propkee, payestka mozhit dleetsa sorak pyat ... asobeenna pa pyatneetsam, kagda khoozhe fseevo. Skol'ka stoeet? Abichna ot treetsatee do peeteedeeseetee rooblyeiy.*

Say it simply

1 You are staying in a hotel in Russia. The television and the shower are both broken. Report it – you want to use both!

2 You are at the airport, about to catch your flight home when you realize that you have left a bag behind in the room of your hotel. You phone the hotel reception and ask for it to be sent on to you.

What would you say in these two cases? Say it then write it down. Then see the two examples in the **Answers** section. Give it a go!

Let's speak Russian

◀) CD2, tr 25

Here's a quick warm-up. Answer the questions using the words in brackets.

1 On koopeel dom v Marbella? (da, paneedyel'neek)
2 Skol'ka lyet vi rabotalee v bankee? (pyat)
3 Kagda vi gavareelee s vashiiy feermaiy? (fcheera)
4 Pacheemoo vam nada atryemanteeravat' vashoo mashinoo? (patamoo shta, ana staraya)
5 On bil snachala v gasteeneetsi? (nyet, f kvarteeree)

Now practise your verbs with nada, neelzya and para:

6 Oozhas! Kvarteera ocheen' staraya... (You mustn't buy it.)
7 Skaryeye! Oozhe dyeveet' cheesof... (It's time for us to go.)
8 ... (You must mend the television), yeslee on nee rabotaeet.

Finish off the sentences, using phrases which start with shto and patamoo shta:

9 Maya padrooga skazala... (that already end of holiday).
10 Eeshshyo ana skazala... (that she really likes Moscow).
11 Maya zhina khocheet skazat'... (that she has (a) cold).
12 Moiy moosh gavareet, shto on nee mozhit f tyatr... (because he is working).
13 Ol'ga tozhe ne mozhit f tyatr... (because she is on holiday).
14 Moiy droog gavareet... (that she is very beautiful).
15 On gavareet tozhe... (that he wants her telephone number).

Answers

1 Da, on koop**ee**l dom v Marbella f paneed**yel**'neek.

2 Ya rab**o**tal/rab**o**tala v b**a**nkee pyat lyet.

3 Ya gavar**ee**l/gavar**ee**la s ma**yeiy fee**rmaiy fcheer**a**.

4 Nam n**a**da atreemant**ee**ravat' mashin**oo**, patam**oo** shta an**a** st**a**raya.

5 Nyet, snach**a**la on bil f kvart**ee**ree.

6 **Oo**zhas! Kvart**ee**ra **o**cheen' st**a**raya. Vam nee n**a**da ye**yo**.

7 Skar**ye**ye! Oozh**e** d**ye**veet chees**o**f. Nam par**a** eet**ee**.

8 Vam n**a**da atreemant**ee**ravat' teeleev**ee**zar, **ye**slee on nee rab**o**taeet.

9 Ma**ya** padr**oo**ga skaz**a**la, shto oozh**e** kan**ye**ts **o**tpooska.

10 Eeshshyo an**a** skaz**a**la, shto yeiy ocheen' nr**a**veetsa Maskv**a**.

11 Ma**ya** zhin**a** kh**o**ch'eet skaz**a**t', shto oo nee**yo** prast**oo**da.

12 Moiy moosh gavar**ee**t, shto on nee m**o**zhit v **tya**tr, patam**oo** shta on rab**o**tayet.

13 **O**l'ga t**o**zhe ne m**o**zhit f **tya**tr, patam**oo** shta an**a** v **o**tpooskye.

14 Moiy droog gavar**ee**t, shto an**a o**cheen' kras**ee**vaya.

15 On gavar**ee**t t**o**zhe, shto on kh**o**cheet yee**yo** n**o**meer teeleef**o**na.

Let's speak more Russian

◀) CD2, tr 26

In your own words

This exercise will teach you to express yourself freely. Use only the words you have learned so far.

Tell me in your own words that...

1 tomorrow is the end of your holiday
2 nobody knows where you have been
3 next year you are going on a ship to Saint-Petersburg
4 your mother knows the number of your mobile phone
5 you are going to Novgorod on the train; it is cheaper
6 now you know Tver well
7 at Christmas you are going to your friend in England
8 his wife works in Moscow
9 your children were with (by) him in the flat
10 you like the restaurant

Answers

1 Zaftra kanyets nashiva otpooska.
2 Neekto nye znaeet, gdye mi bilee.
3 V slyedooyshsheem gadoo mi payedeem na teeplakhodee f Sankt-Peeteerboork.
4 Mama znaeet nomeer nashiva sotavava teeleefona.
5 Mi yedeem v Novgarat na poeezdee, tak deeshevlee.
6 Seechas mi kharasho znaeem Tvyer.
7 Na Razhdeestvo mi payedeem g droogoo v Angleeyu.
8 Yeevo zhina rabotaeet v Maskvye.
9 Nashi dyetee bilee oo neevo v kvarteeree.
88 10 Mnye nraveetsa reestaran.

Let's speak Russian – fast and fluently

🔊 CD2, tr 27

Translate each section and check if it is correct. Then cover the answers and say the sentences as quickly as you can!

I want to (go to) Hawaii for several days.
We have never been in Moscow.
In my firm they know the number of my mobile phone.

Ya khach**u** na Gav**ai**yee na n**ye**skal'ka dny**ei**y.
Mi neekagd**a** nye b**i**lee v Maskv**ye**.
V ma**yei**y f**ee**rmee zn**a**yut n**o**meer s**o**tavava teelef**o**na.

The girlfriend invites me to Greece on the boat.
It is interesting, but expensive costs. Cheaper to buy ticket to Sochi.
There by us beautiful house.

Padr**oo**ga preeglash**a**eet meen**ya** v Gr**ye**tsiyu na teeplakh**o**dee.
Eta eenteer**ye**sna, no d**o**raga st**o**eet. Deesh**e**vlee koop**ee**t' beel**yet**
f S**o**chee.
Tam oo nas kras**ee**viy dom.

What are you doing here? My husband wants to buy computer.
You can't us help? Here nothing suitable not.
Downstairs can buy cheaper.

Shto vi z'dyes' d**ye**laeetee? Moiy moosh kh**o**cheet koop**ee**t'
kamp'**yu**tir.
Vi n**ye** m**o**zhitee nam pam**o**ch'? Z'dyes' neecheev**o** padhad**ya**shsheeva
nyet.
Vneez**oo** m**o**zhna koop**ee**t' deesh**e**vlee.

Now say all the sentences in Russian without stopping and starting.

Test your progress

A lot of verbs have been included in this test. But don't panic – it looks worse than it is. Go for it – you'll do brilliantly.

1 I like writing letters because I have (a) new computer.
2 How are you? You have (a) problem? To help you (Can I help you?).
3 Excuse me, do you have the number of (her) mobile?
4 I like (the) Crimea (Krim). It is never cold there.
5 The other case is in (the) bus. Have you got (the) brown bag?
6 Where will you be at Christmas?
7 Who wants fish and who wants meat?
8 He has my telephone number. He often rings me.
9 Quickly! Where is (the) ticket? The train is coming!
10 Don't you know that (the) airport is always open?
11 My holiday is very important. I want (to go) to Italy.
12 Have you seen Olga in the newspaper? Without (her) husband?
13 Your mother is very pleasant. Her walnut cake is delicious!
14 We must work. We have three boys and one girl. Very expensive costs!
15 Excuse me, where is it possible to repair (the) car?
16 I know him. He always goes shopping with (his) dog.
17 Who said it is impossible (one cannot) here to smoke?
18 We are travelling to (the) airport by taxi, then to Dallas by plane.
19 I would like to speak to (the) waiter. Where is (the) bill?
20 I am sorry, but this is the end of **Fast Russian with Elisabeth Smith**.

Check your answers, then enter your final excellent score on the **Progress chart** and write out your certificate!

Answers

How to score

From a total of 100%

- Subtract 1% for each wrong or missing word.
- Subtract 1% for the wrong form of the verb, like **yed**eem when it should be **yed**oo.
- Subtract 1% for mixing up the pronouns such as vi, vam, v**a**mee.

There are no penalties for:

- Wrong or different ending of the word, e.g. kamp'yutir – kamp'yutira. In a very few cases you will not already have met the correct word ending that you see in the answer. As long as you have the right word, you're doing fine and will be understood. Remember, near enough is good enough.
- Picking the wrong 'version' of the word, e.g. noviy – novim.
- Picking the wrong word where there are two of similar meaning, e.g. no and a.
- Wrong spelling, as long as you can say the word! e.g. ee**yu**n – iy**oo**n.
- Different word order.

For each test, correct your mistakes. Then read the corrected answers out loud twice.

> **100% MINUS YOUR PENALTIES WILL GIVE YOU YOUR WEEKLY SCORE.**

Week 1: Test your progress

1 Meenya zavoot Frank Lukas.
2 Zdrastvooitee, mi – Veektar ee Ol'ga.
3 Ya tozhe eez Omska.
4 V aktyabrye ya bil/bila v Maskvye.
5 Mi bilee tree goda v Amyereekee.
6 Londan stoeet doraga.
7 Eezveeneetee, pazhaloosta, gdye vi rabotaeetee?
8 Vi rabotaeete v Manchyes'teeree?
9 Vi Veektar Eezmaiylaf ees Tomska?
10 Kvarteera v Novgaradee ocheen' bal'shaya.
11 Meenootachkoo, pazhaloosta, oo meenya bol'shi dyeneek.
12 Tam yes't' teeleefon? Nyet, k sazhilyeneeyu.
13 Ya v Yaltee bees sina.
14 Feerma bal'shaya?
15 Meerseedes doraga stoeet?
16 V apryelee Londan ocheen' kraseeviiy.
17 Oo neevo f tooragyentstvee padrooga.
18 K sazhilyeneeyu rabota ocheen' skoochnaya.
19 Rabota ocheen' kharoshaya, no otpoosk loochshe.
20 Maya doch vseegda zvaneet.

Your score: _____ %

Week 2: Test your progress

1 Ya p'yu mnoga shampanskava.
2 Skol'ka stoeet zaftrak, pazhaloosta.
3 Z'dyes' yes't' tooragyenstva?
4 Oo vas yes't' stol? F syem peetnatsat'?
5 Ya khachu peet' kofee.
6 Moiy otpoosk va Flareedee bil loochshe.
7 Gdye kharoshaya gasteeneetsa?
8 Telefoniy shshyot, pazhaloosta.
9 Mi bilee f Sankt-Peeteerboorgee v maee.
10 Moiy dom sleeshkam bal'shoiy.
11 F katoram chyasoo vi v Maskvoo zaftra?
12 Ya tam s vos'mee do peetee.

13 Eezveen**ee**tee, pazhal**oo**sta. Gdye tooal**ye**ty, pr**ya**ma?

14 Mi khat**ee**m **ye**khat' v Osla v yeenvar**ye**, no sl**ee**shkam kholadna.

15 **E**ta st**oo**eet bol'shi d**ye**neek?

16 Z**a**ftra, gdye vi v d**ye**seet' tr**ee**tsat?

17 Oozh**a**sna. N**o**meer **o**cheen' d**o**raga st**oo**eet.

18 Z'dyes' m**o**zhna peet' k**o**fee seech**ya**s? Oo vas yes't' meest**a**?

19 Oo nas mal**ee**nkieeiy dom v Am**ye**reekee, no on **o**cheen' d**o**raga
st**oo**eet.

20 Da sveed**a**neeya, mi **ye**deem v Yalt**oo**.

> Your score: _____ %

Week 3: Test your progress

1 Gdye pradav**ye**ts?

2 Gdye m**o**zhna koop**ee**t' bootirbr**o**di?

3 Kagd**a** vam n**a**da v Angl**ee**yu seev**o**dnya? F syem' chees**o**f?

4 Mi oov**ee**d**ee**lee **e**ta vch**ee**r**a** po teeleev**ee**zaroo.

5 Seech**ya**s magaz**ee**ni atkr**i**ti, k**a**zhitsa.

6 Z'dyes' yes't' oonee v**ee**rmak **ee**lee soop**ee**rm**a**rkeet?

7 Eezveen**ee**tee, vi t**o**zhe eed**yo**tee na p**o**chtoo?

8 Gdye vi koop**ee**lee angl**ee**sk**o**oyu gaz**ye**too?

9 Vi khat**ee**tye k**o**fee **ee**lee ch**ya**iy?

10 Seev**o**dnya pag**o**da plakh**a**ya. Neel'z**ya** v N**o**vgarat.

11 **E**ta fsyo? **E**ta b**i**la need**o**raga.

12 Mark**ee** st**o**eelee peetn**a**tsat' r**oo**bl**ei**y.

13 Mi preen**ee**m**a**eem kreed**ee**tn**ee**e k**a**rtochkee.

14 Tr**ee**sta gram sira sl**ee**shkam mn**o**ga? Nyet, nyet prabl**ye**m.

15 Yes't' n**o**vaya kh**ee**mch**ee**estka bl**ee**ska ats**yu**da.

16 Oo vas yes't' pak**ye**teek dlya ma**ei**y f**oo**dbolkee, pazhal**oo**sta?

17 Ya z'dyes' oov**ee**d**ee**la apt**ye**koo, k**a**zhitsa.

18 B**o**zhe moiy! Aft**o**boos nee rab**o**taeet ee Meers**ee**d**e**s t**o**zhe nee
rab**o**taeet!

19 Vi oov**ee**d**ee**lee f**oo**dbolk**oo**? Gdye vi koop**ee**lee y**ee**yo?

20 Peets**o**t r**oo**bl**ye**iy, no oo meen**ya** t**o**lka d**o**lari.

> Your score: _____ %

Week 4: Test your progress

1 Ya doomayu, shto fstryechya va ftorneek.
2 Seevodnya? Nyet, eezveeneetee, eta neevazmozhna.
3 Mnye nada koopeet' mnoga padarkaf.
4 Vi nye mozhite mnye pamoch', pazhaloosta? Ya khachu nomeer vrachya.
5 Vi nye znaeete, gdye yes't' kharoshiy reestaran?
6 Tserkaf' ocheen' eentyeryesnaya, kazhitsa.
7 Mi khatyelee bi yekhat' f paneedyel'neek vyecheeram pazhaloosta.
8 Mozhna meenyu, pazhaloosta?
9 Eezveeneetee, pazhaloosta, gdye boomagee?
10 Z'dyes' mozhna koopeet' frookti?
11 Vi znaeete yeevo noviy reestaran?
12 Eta bila preekrasna. Spaseeba balshoye za ocheen' preeyatniy vyecheer.
13 Pacheemoo vam nada veedeet' mayu kreedeetnooyu kartachkoo?
14 Bila skooshna f tyatree f paneedyel'neek.
15 Vi veedeetee teeleefon naveerkhoo, okala vikhada, okala dvyeree.
16 Mi yedeem kooreetsoo eelee kalbasoo... riba sleeshkam doraga stoeet.
17 Kak pa-roosskee...?
18 Vi nee znaeetee, gdye z'dyes' aftoboos?
19 Moiy moosh khocheet yekhat' f Teekhas, a ya khatyela bi yekhat' v N'yu York.
20 On nee znaeet, shto noviy reestaran za tserkav'yu.

Your score: _____%

Week 5: Test your progress

1 Mnye nee nraveetsa eta soomka. Droogaya soomka bila loochshe.
2 Skol'ka stoeet beelyet – tooda ee abratna?
3 Shto vi skazalee? Pamyedleeneeye, pazhaloosta.
4 Ya znayu, shto v Amyereekee beenzeen deeshevlee.
5 V meetro kooreet' zapreeshshaeetsa.
6 Ya nye magoo zhdat'. Oo meenya fstryechya v adeenatsat' cheesof.
7 Eta pachtoviy yashsheek? Zholtiy yashsheek?
8 Allo, mi f treetsatee keelamyetrakh ot Novgarada. Eta benzazaprafka?

9 Shto deeshevlee? Aftoboos eelee meetro?

10 Seev**o**dnya **o**cheen' kh**o**ladna. Nad**y**eyus, b**oo**deet dosht.

11 Sveetaf**o**r bil kr**a**snyiy, nee zeel**yo**nyiy. Vot pacheem**oo** an**ee o**ba v baln**ee**tsi.

12 An**a** bil**a** na benzazapr**a**fkoiy f paneed**ye**l'neek ee va ft**o**rneek. Mash**i**na p'yot beenz**ee**n!

13 Gdye z'des' kheemch**ee**stka? Oo meen**ya** m**a**sla na foodb**o**lkee 'Armanee'.

14 Nasha kvart**ee**ra za gl**a**vnaiy **oo**leetseiy, oo (**or o**kala) astan**o**fkee aft**o**boosa.

15 Mi v meel**ee**tsi-ee, patam**oo** shta mi nee zn**a**eem, gdye moiy s**o**taviy teel**ee**fon.

16 Nada koop**ee**t' beel**y**eti seech**ya**s, patam**oo** shta an**ee** deesh**e**vlee.

17 Mnye nrav**ee**tsa v**a**sha mash**i**na. An**a o**cheen' dor**a**ga st**o**eela?

18 Vi nee m**o**zhitee nam pam**o**ch'? M**o**zhna z'dyes' yes't' **o**kala reek**ee**?

Your score: _____%

Week 6: Quiz
1b, 2c, 3d, 4a, 5d, 6b, 7c, 8b, 9a, 10b/d

Week 6: Spot the keys
Depends when you travel. Usually 20 minutes, but at rush hour when traffic jams everywhere, journey might last 45 minutes. Cost usually between 30 and 50 roubles.

Week 6: Say it simply
1 Eezveen**ee**tee, pazh**a**loosta, ya v n**o**meere 222. Tam teelee**vee**zar nee rab**o**taeet ee doosh nee rab**o**taeet. Pazh**a**loosta, eekh n**a**da atreeman**tee**ravat'. Ya nad**ye**yus, shto vi m**o**zhitee mnye pam**o**ch'!

2 Zdr**a**stvooiytee. Gavar**ee**t Kate Green. Ya bil**a** v v**a**sheiy gast**ee**neetse, v n**o**meeree... K sazhil**ye**neeyu ya oozh**e** v aerapart**oo**, a may**a** s**oo**mka v n**o**meeree. Pazh**a**loosta, may**u** s**oo**mkoo n**a**da v **A**ngleeyu. Gast**ee**neetsa zn**a**eet, gdye ya zhiv**oo**. Spas**ee**ba bal'sh**o**ye.

Test your progress
1 Mnye nrav**ee**tsa pees**a**t' pees'ma, patam**oo** shta oo meen**ya** n**o**viiy kamp'**yu**tir.

2 Kak d**ee**la? Oo vas prabl**ye**ma? Vam pam**o**ch'?

3 Eezveeneetee, oo vas yes't' nomeer yeeyo sotavava teeleefona?

4 Mnye nraveetsa Krim. Tam neekagda nee kholadna.

5 Droogoiy cheemadan v aftoboosee. Oo vas kareechneevaya soomka?

6 Gdye vi boodeetee na Razhdeestvo?

7 Kto khocheet riboo ee kto khocheet myasa?

8 Oo neevo moiy nomeer teeleefona. On chyasta zvaneet mnye.

9 Skaryeye! Gdye beelyet? Poeest eedyot!

10 Vi nee znaeete, shto aeraport vseegda atkrit?

11 Moiy otpoosk ocheen' vazhniy. Ya khachu v Italeeyu.

12 Vi veedeelee Ol'goo v gazyetee? Beez moozha?

13 Vasha mama ocheen' preeyatnaya. Yeeyo aryekhaviy tort ocheen' fkoosniy!

14 Nam nada rabotat'. Oo nas tree mal'cheeka ee adna dyevachka. Ocheen' doraga stoeet!

15 Eezveeneetee, gdye mozhna atreemanteeravat' mashinoo?

16 Mi yeevo znaeem. On vseegda dyelaeet pakoopkee s sabakaiy.

17 Kto skazal, shto z'dyes' neel'zya kooreet'?

18 Mi yedeem v aeraport na taksee, patom v Dallas na samalyotee.

19 Ya khachu gavareet' s afeetseeantam. Gdye shshyot?

20 Eezveeneetee, no eta kanyets **Fast Russian with Elisabeth Smith**.

Your score: _____ %

Russian–English dictionary

In this section you'll find all the **New words** that you have learned, including the 'extras', in alphabetical order.

To make it easy for you to find what you may have forgotten, words are shown exactly as they appear in the **New words** section. For example, if you learned *a few* you'll find it under 'a'. If you don't remember how to say *I work* you'll find it under 'I'.

a *and, but*
abratna *back/return*
adeen *one*
adeenatsat' *eleven*
afeetsiant *waiter*
aftoboos/aftoboosee *bus*
aktyabr' *October*
ana *she*
angleeskaya/Angleeya, Anglee-ee *English/England*
apryel' *April*
aptyeka/aptyekoo *chemist's*
aranzhiviiy *orange*
aryekhaviy tort *walnut cake*
astanofka *bus stop*
atkhadeet'/atkhodeet *to leave/it leaves*
atkooda *from where*
atkriti *open (plural form)*
atreemanteeravat' *to repair*
atsyuda *from here*
avgoost *August*

bal'na *ill, sick*
bal'neetsa/bal'neetsoo *hospital*
bal'shaya *big*
baleet *it hurts*
bank/v bankee *bank/in, at bank*
banka/bankoo *tin, jar*
bar *bar*
beefshteks *steak*
beelyet/beelyety *ticket/tickets*
beenzazaprafka *petrol station (colloquial)*
beenzeen *petrol*
bees teeleefona *without telephone*
bil *was*
bilee *were*
bleeska *close, near*
bol'shi *more*
boodoo/boodeet *I will be/he (she, it) will be*
boomaga/boomagee *paper*

97

bootilkoo shampanskava *bottle of champagne*

bootirbrot/bootirbrodi *sandwich/sandwiches*

Bozhe moiy! *Good grief! (lit: God my!)*

broshka/broshkoo *brooch*

byeliiy *white*

cheelavyek *person*

cheemadan/ cheemadanam *suitcase*

cheesi *clock*

cheestiee *clean*

cheetiree *four*

cheetireesta *four hundred*

cheetirnatsat' *fourteen*

cheetvyerk *Thursday*

chyaiy *tea*

chyas *hour*

chyasta *often*

chyorniiy *black*

da *yes*

da kakova chyasa? *until when?*

da sveedaneeya *goodbye*

dachya *summer house*

daiytee *give!*

deekabr' *December*

deeshyevlee *cheaper*

deeveenosta *ninety*

deeveetnatsat' *nineteen*

dlya *for*

dlya meenya *for me*

98 dnyeiy/dnya *days*

do, da *until*

dobraye ootra *good morning*

dobriiy dyen' *good day, good afternoon*

dobriiy vyecheer *good evening*

doch *daughter*

dom *house*

doomat'/doomayu *to think/ I think*

doosh (z dooshim) *shower (with a shower)*

doraga *expensive*

droog/droogoo *friend*

droogoiy *other, another*

dva *two*

dva beelyeta *two tickets*

dvatsat' *twenty*

dveenatsat' *twelve*

dvye *(f.) two*

dvyer/dveeree *door*

dvyes'tee *two hundred*

dyela *matter*

dyelat' *to do*

dyen' *day*

dyeneek *money*

dyeseet' *ten*

dyetee *children*

dyevachka/dyevachkee *(little) girl/girls*

dyeveet'/deeveetee *nine*

ee *and*

eedyot *(he, she) it goes, is going*

eedyot dosht' *it's raining*

eekra/eekri *caviar*

eelee *or*
eem *to them*
eenteer**ye**sna *it is interesting*
eeyul' *July*
ee**yu**n' *June*
eez, ees *from*
eezveen**ee** *I am sorry (informal)*
eezveen**ee**tee *excuse me*
eta *it is*
etat/**e**ta *this*

f k**a**toram chees**oo**? *at what time?*
f pyat chees**o**f *at five o'clock*
f sl**ye**dooshshee/**e**tam gad**oo** *next/this year*
f syem' treetsat' *at 7.30*
f tree cheesa *at three o'clock*
fatagr**a**fiya/fatagr**a**feeiy *photograph/photographs*
f**ee**rma/f**ee**rmi *firm*
f**ee**rmeeniee bl**yu**da *firm's dishes (i.e. specials)*
feevr**a**l' *February*
foodb**o**lka *T-shirt*
fr**oo**kt *fruit*
fstr**ye**chya *meeting*
fsyo *all, everything*
ft**o**rneek/ft**o**rneeka *Tuesday*

gaspad**ee**n *Mr*
gaspazh**a** *Mrs*
g**a**tovi *ready*
Gav**a**iyee *Hawaii*

gavar**ee**t'/gavar**ee**t *to speak, to say/he speaks, he says*
gaz**ye**ta *newspaper*
gdye *where*
gl**a**vnaia **oo**leetsa *main street*
g**o**da/g**o**t *year*
g**o**rad, g**o**rat *town*
g**o**t *year*
gr**ee**l'/gr**ee**lya *grill*

iksk**oo**rseeya *excursion*
It**a**leeya/v It**a**leeyu *Italy/ to Italy*

k sazhil**ye**neeyu *unfortunately*
kaf**e** *café*
kagd**a** *when*
kak deel**a**? *how are things?*
kak pa-**roo**skee? *how in Russian?*
kak**oiy**-ta *some (sort of)*
kalbas**a**/kalbas**oo** *sausage*
kamp'**yu**tir/kamp'**yu**tiri *computer*
kan**ye**shna *of course*
kan**ye**ts *end, direction (one way)*
kar**ee**chneeviiy *brown*
k**a**zhitsa *it seems, I think/ believe*
khal**o**dniy *cold*
kharash**o** *good, well*
khar**o**chaya *good*
kheemch**ee**stka/ kheemch**ee**stkoo *dry cleaner's*

99

kholadna *cold*
kleeyent *customer*
kneega *book*
kofee *coffee*
koncheelsa/koncheelas'
   has finished
koopeela *I bought*
koopeet'/koopeela *to buy/*
   she bought
kooreet' *to smoke*
kooreetsa/kooreetsi
   chicken
koosocheek *piece*
krasaveets *handsome fellow*
kraseeviiy *beautiful*
krasniiy *red*
kreedeetniee kartachkee
   credit cards
kto *who*
kto takoiy… ? *who is… ?*
kto-ta *someone*
kvarteera *flat*

Lada/Ladoo *Lada*
loochshe *better*
lyet *of years*

Madyeiyra/Madyeiyroo
   Madeira
magazeen/magazeenee
   shop/shops
maiy *May*
mal'cheek *boy*
mala *few, little*
malako/malakom *milk*
maleen'keeiy/
   maleen'kaya *small*
mami/mama *mother*

markee/markamee *stamps*
mart *March*
mashina *car*
masla *oil*
matryoshka/matryoshkee
   Russian doll/dolls
maya, moiy *my*
meeleetsiya *police*
meenoota *minute*
meenootachkoo *little minute*
meenya zavoot *they call me*
   (I am called)
meenyu *menu*
meesta *places, seats*
mi *we*
mi khateem *we want*
mnoga *many*
moosh *husband*
moozyeiy/moozyeya
   museum
mozhit bit' *perhaps*
mozhna *it is possible*
myasa *meat*
myedleena *slowly*
myeseets *month*
Myeseetsi *months*

na *for, on*
na adnoo noch *for one night*
na cheelavyeka *for a person*
   (per person)
na desyatam itazhe *on the*
   tenth floor
nada *it is necessary*
nadyeyatsa/nadyeyus'
   to hope/I hope
nalyeva *to the left, on the left*
nam *for us*

naprava *to the right, on the right*

naveerkhoo *upstairs*

nayabr' *November*

nee daleeko *it is (not) far, (not) distant*

nee gadeetsa *it does not fit (it's not on)*

nee rabotaeet *does not work*

neecheestaya *not clean*

neecheevo *nothing*

needyelya *week*

neekagda nee *never*

neekooryashshiye *non-smokers*

neekto *no one*

neel'zya *it is not possible, one may not*

neemnoshka *a little*

neeplakhoye *not bad*

no *but*

nomeer *number*

nomeer na dvaeekh *room for two (i.e. double room)*

noo... *well...*

noviy/novim *new*

nye *not*

nye pravda lee *isn't it?*

nyeskal'ka *a few*

nyet *no*

nyet prablyem! *no problem!*

oba *both*

ocheen' *very*

okala *near, by*

on *it/he*

on/yevo/neem *he, him*

oo meenya *I have*

oo nas *by us (we have)*

oo neeyo *she has*

ooneeveermag/ ooneeveermagee *department store*

ooveedeet'/ooveedeela *to see/she saw*

oozhasnaya, oozhasniiy *terrible*

oozhe *already*

pa beeznisoo *on business*

pa vaskreesyeneeyam *on Sundays*

pachemoo *why*

pachtoviy yashsheek *post box*

padarkee/padarkaf *presents*

padazhdee! *wait!*

padrooga *girlfriend*

pagoda *weather*

pakoopkee *the shopping*

pakyeteek *bag*

pamoch' *to help*

pamyedleeneeye *a little more slowly*

paneedyel'neek *Monday*

para *it is time (to go)*

para/paroo *pair, couple*

pareekmakheerskaya/ pareekmakheer-skooyu *hairdresser's*

patamoo shta *because*

patkhadyashsheeiy/ patkhadyashsheeva *suitable*

patom *then, next*

101

pa**ye**deem *let's go*
pa**ye**stka *journey*
paz**h**aloosta *please*
pazvan**eet**'/pazvan**eel**
    to ring/he rang
peedees**yat** *fifty*
p**ee**s'ma *letters*
p**ee**s'**mo** *letter*
p**ee**shim *we write*
peet'/ya p'yu *to drink/I drink*
peetn**a**tsat' *fifteen*
peets**o**t *five hundred*
p**ee**va *beer*
pl**a**kh**a**ya *bad*
plan g**o**rada *plan of the town*
platf**o**rma/platf**o**rmi
    platform
po, pa *on, along,*
    according to
p**o**chta/p**o**chtoo *post office*
p**o**eest/f p**o**eezdee *train/*
    in the train
p**o**lan *full*
poot'/poot**ee** *way, journey*
p**o**zna *it is late*
pradav**ye**ts *shop assistant*
pragram**ee**st *computer*
    programmer
prakampast**ee**ravat'
    to punch, clip
prashl**o** *it went by, passed*
prast**oo**da *a cold*
preeglashat'/preeglashayu
    to invite/I invite
preek**ra**snaya *splendid*
pre**ee**neemaeem *we accept*
pre**eya**tniiy *pleasant*

pr**ya**ma *straight on*

pyat' *five*
p**ya**tneetsa *Friday*
p**ye**rvyiy *first*

rab**o**ta *work, job*
rab**o**taeetee *you work*
rab**o**tal *I, he worked*
rab**o**tala *I, she worked*
rab**o**tayu *I work*
rad**ee**teelee *parents*
Razhde**e**stv**o** *Christmas*
re**e**k**a** *river*
r**i**ba/r**i**boo *fish*
r**oo**bl**ee**, r**oo**bl**yeiy** *rouble(s)*
r**o**zaviiy *pink*

s **oo**ma s**a**shl**a** *crazy!*
    (to a man one would say:
    *s **oo**ma s**a**shol)*
s v**a**naiy *with a bathroom*
s vas'm**ee** chees**o**f *from*
    eight hours (from eight
    o'clock)
s, z *with, from*
sab**a**ka *dog*
s**a**khar/s**a**khara *sugar*
sal**a**t/sal**a**tam *salad*
samal**yo**t(ee) *aeroplane*
seech**ya**s *now*
seemn**a**tsat' *seventeen*
s**ee**neey *blue*
seent**ya**br' *September*
seev**o**dnya *today*
shamp**a**nskaye *champagne*
shes't' *six*
shik**a**lat *chocolate*
shisn**a**tsat' *sixteen*
shis**o**t *six hundred*

shiz'deesyat *sixty*

shkola *school*

shshyot *bill*

shto *what, that*

sin *son*

sir/siram *cheese*

skaryeye *hurry*

skazat'/skazal *to say/he said*

skol'ka *how much/how many*

skoochnaya *boring*

slamalas' *it has broken down*

slatkaye *sweet, dessert*

sleeshkam *too (as in too much)*

slooshayu *I listen*

slyedooshshyeeiy *next*

smatryet' *to watch*

snachyala *first*

snyat' *to take (of photographs)*

snyek/sneegoo *snow*

sontse *sun*

soobota *Saturday*

soomka, soomkee *bag*

soop *soup*

soopeermarkeet *supermarket*

sooveeneeri/sooveeneeraf *souvenirs*

sorak *forty*

sotaviy (teeleefon) *mobile (telephone)*

spaseeba/balshoiye *thank you/very much*

sport/sporta/sportoo *sport*

sreeda *Wednesday*

S-SHA *USA*

stakan *glass*

stantseeya meetro *metro station*

staroye/staraya *old*

sto *hundred*

stoeet *costs*

stol *table*

sveetafor/sveetafora *traffic lights*

svodyat meenya s ooma *are driving me crazy*

syem' *seven*

syem' sorak pyat' *7.45*

syemdeesyat *seventy*

syeriiy *grey*

tak *thus, so*

takoiy zhe … kak *just as … as*

taksee *taxi*

tam *there*

teeleeveezar/teeleeveezaroo *television*

teeplakhot/teeplakhodee *ship*

tenees *tennis*

tiseechya *thousand*

tol'ka *only*

tooalyeti *toilets*

tooda *to there*

tozhe *also*

tree *three*

tree cheesa *it is three o'clock*

treenatsat' *thirteen*

treesta *three hundred*

treetsat myetraf *30 metres*　　**103**

treetsat' *thirty*
tsentr *centre*
tserkaf'/tserkav'yu *church*
Tsifri *numerals*
Tsveeta *colours*
tyomnava myasa *dark (red) meat*

v avgoos'tee *in August*
v dva cheesa *at two o'clock*
v maee *in May*
v ooneeveerseetyetee *at a/the university*
v otpooskee *on holiday*
v tooragyentstvee *in a/the travel agency*
v, va, f *in, to, at*
vada/vadi *water*
vagzal *(railway) station*
vapros *question*
vaseemnatsat *eighteen*
vaskreesyen'ye *Sunday*
vazhniee *important*
vazmozhna *it is possible*
veetcheena/veetcheenoiy *ham*
veedeet'/veezhoo *to see/ I see*
veeleekalyepna *splendid(ly), great, wonderful(ly)*
veeno *wine*
vi *you (polite)*
vi/vas *you*
vikhad/vikhada *exit*
vizvat' … *to summon, call, send for*
vneezoo *downstairs*

104 von tam *over there*

voseem' *eight*
voseem' peetnatsat' *at 8.15*
voseemdeesyat *eighty*
vot *here (there) is/are*
vrach/vrachya *doctor*
vryedna *it is harmful*
vryemya *time*
Vryemya *telling the time*
vseegda *always*

ya *I*
yantarnaya *amber*
yanvar' *January*
yedeem *we go (travel)*
yedoo *I go (travel)*
yelee *we/they ate*
yes't' *there is/is there*
yuveleerniy *jewellery*

z'dyes' *here*
za *for, behind, beyond*
zaftra *tomorrow*
zaftrak *breakfast*
zaftrakat' *to have breakfast*
zapreeshshaeetsa *it is forbidden*
zdrastvooiytee *hello*
zeelyoniiy *green*
zhareenaiy kartoshkaiy *fried potato*
zhdat' *to wait*
zhina *wife*
zhirna *it is greasy*
zhivyot *lives*
zholtiiy *yellow*
znat'/znayu/znaeet *to know/ I know/he/(she) knows*
zvaneet *rings, phones*

English–Russian dictionary

a few n**ye**skal'ka
a little neemn**o**shka
a little more slowly
  pam**ye**d-le-eneeye
according to po, pa
aeroplane samal**yo**t(ee)
all fsyo
along po, pa
already oozh**e**
also t**o**zhe
always vseegd**a**
amber yant**a**rnaya
and a/ee
another droog**oiy**
April apr**ye**l'
are driving me crazy svodyat
  meen**ya** s oom**a**
at f
at a/the university v
  ooneeveerseet**ye**tee
at five o'clock f pyat
  chees**o**f
at seven thirty f syem'
  tr**ee**t sat'
at three o'clock f tree
  chees**a**
at two o'clock v dva chees**a**
at what time? f kat**o**ram
  chees**oo**?
August **a**vgoost

back abr**a**tna
bad plakh**a**ya
bag pak**ye**teek, s**oo**mka,
  s**oo**mkee
bank/in, at bank bank/
  v b**a**nkee
bar bar
beautiful kras**ee**viiy
because patam**oo** shta
beer p**ee**va
behind za
better l**oo**chshe
beyond za
big bal'sh**a**ya
bill shsh**yo**t
black ch**yo**rniiy
blue s**ee**neey
book kn**ee**ga
boring sk**oo**chnaya
both **o**ba
bottle of champagne
  boot**i**lka shamp
  anskava
boy m**a**l'cheek
breakfast z**a**ftrak
brooch br**o**shka/br**o**shkoo
brown kar**ee**chneeviiy
bus aft**o**boos/aft**o**boosee
bus stop astan**o**fka
but a, no

by okala
by us (we have) oo nas

café kafe
call vizvat' ...
car mashina
caviar eekra/eekri
centre tsentr
champagne shampanskaye
cheaper deeshyevlee
cheese sir/siram
chemist's aptyeka/aptyekoo
chicken kooreetsa/
   kooreetsi
children dyetee
chocolate shikalat
Christmas Razhdeestvo
church tserkaf'/tserkav'yu
clean cheestiee
clip prakampasteeravat'
clock cheesi
close bleeska
coffee kofee
cold prastooda, khalodniy/
   kholadna
colours tsveeta
computer kamp' yutir/
   kamp' yutiri
computer programmer
   pragrameest
costs stoeet
couple paroo
crazy! s ooma sashla
   (to a man one would say:
   s ooma sashol)
credit cards kreedeetniee
   kartachkee

106 *customer* kleeyent

dark (red) meat tyomnava
   myasa
daughter doch
day dyen'
days dnyeiy/dnya
December deekabr'
department store
   ooneeveermag/
   ooneeveermagee
dessert slatkaye
direction (one way)
   kanyets
doctor vrach/vrachya
does not work nee
   rabotaeet
dog sabaka
door dvyer/dveree
downstairs vneezoo
dry cleaner's
   kheemcheestka/
   kheemcheestkoo

eight voseem'
eight fifteen voseem'
   peetnatsat
eighteen vaseemnatsat
eighty voseemdeesyat
eleven adeenatsat'
end, direction (one way)
   kanyets
England Angleeya,
   Anglee-ee
English angleeskaya
everything fsyo
excursion ikskoorseeya
excuse me eezveeneetee
exit vikhad/vikhada
expensive doraga

February feevral'
few mala
fifteen peetnatsat'
fifty peedeesyat
firm feerma/feermi
firm's dishes (i.e. specials)
   feer-meeniee blyuda
first snachyala, pyervyiy
fish riba/riboo
five pyat'
five hundred peetsot
flat kvarteera
for na, za, dlya
for a person (per person)
   na cheelavyeka
for me dlya meenya
for one night na adnoo noch
for us nam
forty sorak
four cheetiree
four hundred cheetireesta
fourteen cheetirnatsat'
Friday pyatneetsa
fried potato zhareenaiy
   kartoshkaiy
friend droog/droogoo
from z, eez, ees
*from eight hours (from
   eight o'clock)* s vas'mee
   cheesof
from here atsyuda
from where atkooda
fruit frookt
full polan

girl/girls (little) dyevachka/
   dyevachkee
girlfriend padrooga

give! daiytee
glass stakan
good kharasho/kharochaya
good afternoon dobriiy
   dyen'
good day dobriiy dyen'
good evening dobriiy
   vyecheer
Good grief! (lit: God my!)
   Bozhe moiy!
good morning dobraye
   ootra
goodbye da sveedaneeya
great veeleekalyepna
green zeelyoniiy
grey syeriiy
grill greel'/greelya

hairdresser's pareekmakheer-
   skaya/
   pareekmakheerskooyu
ham veetcheena/
   veetcheenoiy
handsome fellow krasaveets
has finished koncheelsa/
   koncheelas'
Hawaii Gavaiyee
he on
he goes eedyot
he rang pazvaneel
he said skazal
he says gavareet
he speaks gavareet
he worked rabotal
he/she knows znaeet
hello zdrastvooiytee
here z'dyes'
here is/are vot

107

him yevo, neem
hospital bal'neetsa/
  bal'neetsoo
hour chyas
house dom
how are things? kak deela?
how in Russian? kak
  pa-rooskee?
how many skol'ka
how much skol'ka
hundred sto
hurry skaryeye
husband moosh

I ya
I am sorry (informal) eezve-
  enee
I believe kazhitsa
I bought koopeela
I drink ya p'yu
I go (travel) yedoo
I have oo meenya
I invite preeglashayu
I know znayu
I listen slooshayu
I see veezhoo
I think doomayu, kazhitsa
*I will be/he (she, it) will
  be* boodoo/boodeet
I work rabotayu
I worked rabotala, rabotal
ill bal'na
important vazhniee
in v, va, f
in a/the travel agency
  v tooragyentstvee
in August v avgoos'tee
108 *in May* v maee

in the train f poeezdee
is going eedyot
is there yes't'
isn't it? nye pravda lee
it on
it does not fit (it's not on)
  nee gadeetsa
it goes eedyot
it has broken down
  slamalas'
it hurts baleet
it is eta
it is (not) far, (not) distant
  nee daleeko
it is forbidden
  zapreeshshaeetsa
it is greasy zhirna
it is harmful vryedna
it is interesting eenteeryesna
it is late pozna
it is necessary nada
it is not possible neel'zya
it is possible vazmozhna,
  mozhna
it is raining eedyot dosht'
it is three o'clock tree
  cheesa
it is time (to go) para
it leaves atkhodeet
it seems kazhitsa
it went by prashlo
Italy/to Italy Italeeya/
  v Italeeyu

January yanvar'
jar banka/bankoo
jewellery yuveleerniy
job rabota

journey pa**ye**stka, poot**ee**,
  poot'
July eeyul'
June ee**yu**n'
just as… as tak**oiy** zhe…
  kak

Lada **L**ada/**L**adoo
let's go pa**ye**deem
letter/letters pees'm**o**/
  p**ee**s'ma
little m**a**la
little minute meen**oo**tachkoo
lives zhivy**ot**

Madeira Mad**yeiy**ra/
  Mad**yeiy**roo
main street gl**a**vnaiy **oo**leetsi
many mn**o**ga
March mart
matter d**ye**la
May m**a**iy
meat m**y**asa
meeting fstr**ye**chya
menu meen**yu**
metro station st**a**ntseeya
  meetr**o**
milk malak**o**/malak**o**m
minute meen**oo**ta
mobile (telephone) s**o**taviy
  (teeleef**o**n)
Monday paneed**ye**l'neek
money d**ye**neek
month/s m**ye**seets/
  M**ye**seetsi
more b**o**l'shi
mother m**a**mi/m**a**ma
Mr gaspad**ee**n

Mrs gaspazh**a**
museum mooz**yeiy**/
  mooz**ye**ya
my m**a**ya, moiy

near bl**ee**ska, **o**kala
never neekagd**a** nee
new n**o**viy/n**o**vim
newspaper gaz**ye**ta
next pat**o**m,
  sl**ye**dooshshyeeiy
next/this year f
  sl**ye**dooshshee/**e**tam
  gad**oo**
nine d**ye**veet'/deeveet**ee**
nineteen deeveetn**a**tsat'
ninety deeveen**o**sta
no nyet
no one neekt**o**
no problem! nyet prabl**ye**m!
non-smokers neekoor**ya**s-
  hshiye
not nye
not bad neeplakh**o**ye
not clean neech**ee**staya
nothing neechev**o**
November na**ya**br'
now seechy**a**s
number n**o**meer
numerals ts**i**fri

October akt**ya**br'
of course kan**ye**shna
of years lyet
often chy**a**sta
oil m**a**sla
old st**a**roye/st**a**raya
on na, po, pa

on business pa b**ee**znisoo
on holiday v **o**tpooskee
on Sundays pa vaskreesy**e**-
   neeyam
on the left nal**ye**va
on the right napr**a**va
on the tenth floor na
   des**ya**tam itazh**e**
one ad**ee**n
one may not neel'z**ya**
only t**o**l'ka
open (plural form) atkr**i**ti
or **ee**lee
orange ar**a**nzhiviiy
other droog**oiy**
over there von tam

pair p**a**ra
paper boom**a**ga/boom**a**gee
parents rad**ee**teelee
passed prashl**o**
perhaps m**o**zhit bit'
person cheelav**ye**k
petrol beenz**ee**n
petrol station (colloquial)
   been-zazapr**a**fka
phones zvan**ee**t
photograph/photographs
   fata-gr**a**fiya/fatagraf**ee**iy
piece koos**o**cheek
pink r**o**zaviiy
places meest**a**
plan of the town plan g**o**rada
platform platf**o**rma/
   platf**o**rmi
pleasant pre**eya**tniiy
please pazh**a**loosta
110 *police* meel**ee**tsiya

post box pacht**o**viy
   yashsheek
post office p**o**chta/p**o**chtoo
presents pad**a**rkee/pad**a**rkaf

question vapr**o**s

ready gat**o**vi
red kr**a**sniiy
return abr**a**tna
rings zvan**ee**t
river reek**a**
room for two (i.e. double
   room) n**o**meer na
   dva**ee**kh
rouble(s) roobl**ee**, roobl**yeiy**
Russian doll/dolls
   matr**yo**shka/matr**yo**shkee

salad sal**a**t/sal**a**tam
sandwich/
   sandwiches bootirbr**o**t/
   bootirbr**o**di
Saturday soob**o**ta
sausage kalbas**a**/kalbas**oo**
school shk**o**la
seats meest**a**
send for vizvat' …
September seent**ya**br'
seven syem'
seven forty-five syem'
   s**o**rak pyat'
seventeen seemn**a**tsat'
seventy s**ye**mdeesyat
she an**a**
she bought koop**ee**la
she goes eed**yo**t
she has oo nee**yo**

she knows zn**a**eet
she saw ooveedeela
she worked rab**o**tala
ship teeplakh**o**t/
 teeplakh**o**dee
shop assistant pradav**ye**ts
shop/shops magaz**ee**n/
 magaz**ee**nee
shopping, the shopping
 pak**oo**pkee
shower (with a shower)
 doosh (z d**oo**shim)
sick bal'n**a**
six sh**e**s't'
six hundred shis**o**t
sixteen shisn**a**tsat'
sixty shiz'dees**ya**t
slowly m**ye**dleena
small mal**ee**n'keeiy/
 mal**ee**n'kaya
snow snyek/sneeg**oo**
so tak
some (sort of) kak**oi**y-ta
someone kto-ta
son sin
soup soop
souvenirs sooveen**ee**ri/
 sooveen**ee**raf
splendid preekr**a**snaya
splendidly veeleekal**ye**pna
sport sp**o**rt/sp**o**rta/sp**o**rtoo
stamps m**a**rkee/m**a**rkamee
station (railway) vagz**a**l
steak beefsht**e**ks
straight on pr**ya**ma
sugar s**a**khar/s**a**khara
suitable patkhad**ya**shsheeiy/
 patkhad**ya**shsheeva

suitcase cheemad**a**n/
 cheemad**a**nam
summer house d**a**chya
sun s**o**ntse
Sunday vaskrees**ye**n'ye
supermarket
 soopeerm**a**rkeet
sweet sl**a**tkaye

table stol
taxi taks**ee**
tea chyaiy
television teeleev**ee**zar/
 teeleev**ee**zaroo
telling the time skaz**a**t
 vr**ye**mya
ten d**ye**seet'
tennis t**e**nees
terrible oozh**a**snaya,
 oozh**a**sniiy
thank you/very much
 spas**ee**ba/balsh**oi**ye
that shto
then pat**o**m
there tam
there is yes't'
there is/are vot
they ate **ye**lee
they call me (I am called)
 meen**ya** zav**oo**t
thirteen treen**a**tsat'
thirty tr**ee**tsat'
thirty metres tr**ee**tsat
 m**ye**traf
this **e**tat/**e**ta
thousand t**i**seechya
three tree
three hundred tr**ee**sta

Thursday cheetv**ye**rk
thus tak
ticket/tickets beel**ye**t/
 beel**ye**ty
time vr**ye**mya
tin b**a**nka/b**a**nkoo
to va
to buy koop**ee**t'
to do d**ye**lat'
to drink peet'
to have breakfast z**a**ftrakat'
to help pam**o**ch'
to hope/I hope nad**ye**yatsa/
 nad**ye**yus'
to invite preeglash**a**t'
to know znat'/zn**a**yu/zn**a**eet
to leave atkh**a**deet'
to punch
 prakampast**ee**ravat'
to repair atreemant**ee**ravat'
to ring pazvan**ee**t'
to say skaz**a**t'
to see oov**ee**deet', v**ee**deet'
to smoke koor**ee**t'
to speak gavar**ee**t'/gavar**ee**t
to summon v**i**zvat' ...
to take (of photographs)
 snyat'
to the left nal**ye**va
to the right napr**a**va
to them eem
to there tood**a**
to think d**oo**mat'
to wait zhdat'
to watch smatr**ye**t'
today seev**o**dnya
toilets too**a**lyeti
112 *tomorrow* **za**ftra

too (as in too much)
 sl**ee**shkam
town g**o**rad, g**o**rat
traffic lights sveetaf**o**r/
 sveetaf**o**ra
train p**o**eest
T-shirt foodb**o**lka
Tuesday ft**o**rneek/ft**o**rneeka
twelve dveen**a**tsat'
twenty dv**a**tsat'
two dva, dvye (f)
two hundred dv**ye**s'tee
two tickets dva beel**ye**ta

unfortunately k
 sazhil**ye**neeyu
until do, da
until when? da kak**o**va
 ch**ya**sa?
upstairs naveerkh**oo**
USA S-SHA

very **o**cheen'

wait! pad**a**zhdee!
waiter af**ee**tsiant
walnut cake ar**ye**khaviy tort
was bil
water vad**a**/vad**i**
way poot'
we mi
we accept preeneem**a**eem
we ate **ye**lee
we go (travel) **ye**deem
we want mi khat**ee**m
we write p**ee**shim
weather pag**o**da
Wednesday sreed**a**

week need**ye**lya
well kharash**o**
well ... noo...
were b**i**lee
what shto
when kagd**a**
where gdye
white b**ye**liiy
who kto
who is... ? kto tak**oiy** ... ?
why pachem**oo**
wife zhin**a**
wine veen**o**

with s
with a bathroom s v**a**naiy
without telephone bees
    teeleef**o**na
wonderful(ly)
    veeleekal**ye**pna
work rab**o**ta

year g**o**da/got
yellow zh**o**ltiiy
yes da
you (polite)/you vi/vas
you work rab**o**taeetee

How to use the flash cards

Learning words and sentences can be tedious, but with flash cards it's quick and good fun.

This is what you do

When the **Day-by-day guide** tells you to use the cards, cut them out, photocopy them or copy them on to card. There are 22 **Flash words** and 10 **Flash sentences** for each week. Each card has a little number on it telling you to which week it belongs, so you won't cut out too many cards at a time or muddle them up later on.

First, try to learn the words and sentences by looking at both sides of the cards. Then, when you have a rough idea, start testing yourself. That's the fun bit. Look at the English, say the Russian, and then check. Make a pile each for the 'correct', 'wrong' and 'don't know' ones. When all the cards are used up, start again with the 'wrong' pile and try to whittle it down until you get all of them right. You can also play it 'backwards' by starting with the Russian face-up.

Take them with you on the bus, the train, to the hairdresser's or the dentist's. Do a quick 'turn and learn' wherever you have a bit of spare time.

The 22 **Flash words** for each week are there to start you off. Convert the rest of the **New words** to **Flash words**, too. It's well worth it!

> **Flash cards for 'fast' learning:**
> **Don't lose them – use them!**

eezvee-neetee [1]	pazhaloosta [1]
oo nas [1]	da [1]
mi [1]	nyet [1]
ya [1]	yedoo [1]
vi [1]	rabotayu [1]
gdye [1]	rabota [1]

please [1]	excuse me [1]
yes [1]	by us (we have) [1]
no [1]	we [1]
I go (travel) [1]	I [1]
I work [1]	you [1]
work, job [1]	where [1]

Cut out and use ✂

kharoshiy/ kharoshaya 1	**dyeneek** 1
oo meenya 1	**eta** 1
bank, банк 1	**v otpooskee** 1
dom 1	**vseegda** 1
gorat 1	**sotaviy teeleefon** 1
nada 2	**skol'ka** 2

Cut out and use ✂

money [1]	good [1]
it is [1]	I have [1]
on holiday [1]	bank [1]
always [1]	house [1]
mobile phone [1]	town [1]
how much/ how many [2]	it is necessary [2]

Cut out and use ✂

2 **rooblyeiy**	2 **na cheelavyeka**
2 **kreedeetniee kartachkee**	2 **zaftrak**
2 **mi khateem**	2 **mozhna**
2 **chyaiy**	2 **z'dyes'**
2 **bleeska**	2 **naprava**
2 **vi, vas**	2 **fsyo**

2 **per person**	2 **roubles**
2 **breakfast**	2 **credit cards**
2 **it is possible**	2 **we want**
2 **here**	2 **tea**
2 **on the right**	2 **near**
2 **all, everything**	2 **you**

Cut out and use ✂

oozhasniiy [2]	maleen'keeiy [2]
tooalyeti, M (gents), Ж (ladies) [2]	shshyot [2]
zaftra [2]	pryama [2]
stol [2]	mnoga [2]
na [3]	aftoboos(ee) [3]
plakhaya [3]	pochta/ pochtoo, почта [3]

Cut out and use ✂

small 2	**terrible** 2
bill 2	**toilets** 2
straight on 2	**tomorrow** 2
much, many 2	**table** 2
bus 3	**on, by** 3
post office 3	**bad** 3

Cut out and use ✂

3 **markee**	3 **neel'zya**
3 **soomka**	3 **ooneeveer-mag**
3 **magazeen/ee**	3 **atkrit(i)**
3 **nyet prablyem**	3 **koopeet'**
3 **shto**	3 **neemnoshka**
3 **gazyeta**	3 **vot**

Cut out and use ✂

it's not possible 3	**stamps** 3
department store 3	**bag** 3
open 3	**shop/s** 3
to buy 3	**no problem!** 3
a little 3	**what/that** 3
here is, here are 3	**newspaper** 3

Cut out and use ✂

eedyot 3	**pagoda** 3
pakoopkee 3	**padarkee** 3
preekrasnaya 3	**kholadna** 3
kto-ta 4	**pachemoo** 4
nomeer 4	**kleeyent** 4
kharasho 4	**vazhniee** 4

Cut out and use ✂

3 **weather**	3 **(he, she, it) goes**
3 **presents**	3 **shopping**
3 **cold**	3 **splendid**
4 **why**	4 **someone**
4 **client**	4 **number**
4 **important**	4 **good, well**

Cut out and use ✂

4 **kanyeshna**	4 **eenteeryesna**
4 **kagda**	4 **spaseeba balshoie**
4 **prastooda**	4 **vrach/ vrachya**
4 **riba/riboo**	4 **beefshteks**
4 **peeva**	4 **stakan**
4 **vada/vadi**	4 **neekto**

Cut out and use ✂

it is interesting [4]	of course [4]
thank you very much [4]	when [4]
doctor [4]	cold [4]
steak [4]	fish [4]
glass [4]	beer [4]
no one [4]	water [4]

Cut out and use ✂

4 **naveerkhoo**	4 **okala**
4 **kooreetsa**	4 **pozna**
5 **vagzal, вокзал**	5 **abratna**
5 **poeest**	5 **zapree-shshaeetsa**
5 **mala**	5 **pees'mo**
5 **pachtoviy yashsheek**	5 **oba**

4 **near, by**	4 **upstairs**
4 **it is late**	4 **chicken**
5 **back/return**	5 **(railway) station**
5 **it is forbidden**	5 **train**
5 **letter**	5 **few, little**
5 **both**	5 **post box**

Cut out and use ✂

5 **pyervyiy**	5 **polan**
5 **droogoiy**	5 **etat/eta**
5 **mashina**	5 **staroye/ staraya**
5 **astanofka aftoboosa, остановка**	5 **glavnaiya ooleetsa**
5 **myedleena**	5 **meeleetsiya**
5 **skaryeye!**	5 **eedyot dosht'**

Cut out and use

5	5
full	**first**
this	**other, another**
old	**car**
main street	**bus stop**
police	**slowly**
it's raining	**hurry!**

Cut out and use ✂

5 **shkola**	5 **bal'neetsa**
6 **Razhdeestvo**	6 **snyek/ sneegoo**
6 **payedeem**	6 **teeplakhot**
6 **S-SHA**	6 **veeleekal- yepna**
6 **chyasta**	6 **vneezoo**
6 **aeraport, аэропорт**	6 **neecheevo**

Cut out and use ✀

5	5
hospital	**school**

6	6
snow	**Christmas**

6	6
ship	**let's go**

6	6
great, wonderful	**USA**

6	6
downstairs	**often**

6	6
nothing	**airport**

Cut out and use ✂

6 **dyetee**	6 **mal'cheek**
6 **dyevachka**	6 **kneega**
6 **neekagda nee**	6 **radeeteelee**
6 **droog/ droogoo**	6 **para**
6 **kak deela?**	6 **padazhdee!**
6 **slyedoosh-shee**	6 **moosh**

Cut out and use ✂

6 **boy**	6 **children**
6 **book**	6 **(little) girl**
6 **parents**	6 **never**
6 **it's time (to go)**	6 **friend**
6 **wait!**	6 **how's things?**
6 **husband**	6 **next**

Cut out and use ✂

Meenya zavoot John.

1

Ya bil v Novgaradee.

1

pa beeznisoo

1

Oo meenya kvarteera.

1

Ya rabotayu v Londanee.

1

Oo nas sin ee doch.

1

Gdye vi rabotaeetee?

1

Mi yedeem v Maskvoo.

1

Rabota kharoshaya.

1

Vi v otpooskee?

1

Cut out and use

My name is John. 1

I was in Novgorod. 1

on business 1

I have a flat. 1

I work in London. 1

We have a son and a daughter. 1

Where do you work? 1

We are going to Moscow. 1

The work is good. 1

Are you on holiday? 1

Cut out and use ✂

Oo vas yes't' nomeer? 2

On nye rabotaeet. 2

Skol'ka stoeet? 2

S vasmee da deeveetee. 2

Eta sleeshkam doraga! 2

Mi khateem v Novgarat. 2

Mi khateem bootirbrodi. 2

Z'dyes' yes't'...? 2

Gdye kafe? 2

F katoram cheesoo? 2

Cut out and use

Do you have a room? 2

He isn't working. 2

How much is it? 2

From eight until nine. 2

This/It is too expensive! 2

We want to go to Novgorod. 2

We want some sandwiches. 2

Here there is...? 2

Where is the café? 2

At what time? 2

Cut out and use ✂

Seevodnya nam nada dyelat' pakoopkee. 3

Gdye z'dyes' aftoboos? 3

Golf neel'zya smatryet'. 3

Nam nada v bank. 3

Ya khachu koopeet' foodbolkoo. 3

Eta fsyo. 3

Gde z'dyes' magazeen sooveeneeraf? 3

Magazeeni atkriti da kakova chyasa? 3

Mi mnoga koopeelee. 3

Ocheen' doraga stoeet. 3

Cut out and use

Today we must do/
go shopping   3

Is there a bus here?   3

It is not possible to watch   3
golf.

It is necessary for us   3
(to go) to a bank.

I want to buy a T-shirt.   3

That/It is all.   3

Where is there a souvenir   3
shop?

Shops are open until   3
what time?

We have bought a lot.   3

It is very expensive.   3

Cut out and use ✂

Kto-ta pazvaneel.

4

On nye skazal, pachemoo.

4

Oo meenya fstryechya s neem.

4

Ya yeevo znayu.

4

Tak neel'zya.

4

Shto vi khateetye peet'?

4

Shto vam?

4

Ocheen' vazhniee deela.

4

Vi nye mozhitee mnye pamoch'?

4

Kak pa-rooskee...?

4

Cut out and use

Someone rang. 4

He didn't say why. 4

I have a meeting with him. 4

I know him. 4

One can't do that. 4

What do you want to drink? 4

What would you like? 4

A very important matter. 4

You couldn't help me, 4
could you?

How do you say... 4
in Russian?

Cut out and use ✂

Gdye vagzal? 5

Kagda atkhodeet poeest? 5

**Z'dyes' kooreet'
zapreeshshaeetsa.** 5

Da moozyeya daleeko? 5

Z'dyes' yes't' balneetsa? 5

**Beelyetee nada
prakampasteeravat'.** 5

Mnye nye nraveetsa… 5

**Taksee nee doraga stoeet,
patamoo shta staroye.** 5

Gdye maya soomka? 5

**Ya nadyeyus', shto
prablyem nye boodeet.** 5

Cut out and use

Where is the station? 5

When does the train leave? 5

It is forbidden to smoke here. 5

Is it far to the museum? 5

Is there a hospital here? 5

It is necessary to punch (clip) tickets. 5

I don't like... 5

The taxi is not expensive, because it is old. 5

Where is my bag? 5

I hope that there won't be any problems. 5

Cut out and use ✂

F paneedyelneek mnye **6**
nada boodeet rabotat'.

Ya nee magoo zhdat'. **6**

Gdye vi zhivyotee? **6**

Mnye nada koopeet' **6**
sotaviiy teeleefon.

Oo nas maleen'kaya **6**
kvarteera.

Oozhe kanyets nasheeva **6**
otpooska.

Z'dyes' neecheevo **6**
patkhadyashsheeva nyet.

V etam gadoo... **6**

Kak deela? **6**

Daiytee, pazhaloosta, **6**
gazyetoo.

Cut out and use ✂

On Monday I must work. 6

I can't wait. 6

Where do you live? 6

I must buy a mobile telephone. 6

We have a small flat. 6

Already it is the end of our holiday. 6

There's nothing suitable here. 6

This year… 6

How are you? 6

Please give me the/a newspaper. 6

Cut out and use ✂

*This is to certify
that*

. . . .

*has successfully completed
a six-week course of*

Fast Russian
with Elisabeth Smith

with

. . . .

results

Date . . . .

Author Elizabeth Smith

Praise for Elisabeth Smith

'A language lifeline ... fun, fast and easy.'
(*The Independent*)

'The simple scripts and audio make it crystal clear ... I'm delighted with my progress.'
(*Greece* magazine)

'Its narration is laid-back and encouraging and the method is straightforward. (4-star review)'
(*Time Out*)

'The elements are simple and very straightforward ... strong encouragement ... plenty of opportunity for spoken practice. This course worked very well for me.'
(*Professional Manager* magazine)

'We think it is wonderful.'
(Tom and Maureen Peil, Preston)

'I loved the sense of humour ... Each week I did the final test with bated breath wondering if this time the little bar chart [...] would take a nose dive – but it didn't.'
(Lesly Hopkins, Twickenham)

'This isn't just a package that asks you remember the names for things in a different language this is a package that teaches ... Highly recommended.'
(Maximus)

'It really is an effective way to learn.'
(Mr R. Ellor)

'A solid product offering excellent value for money ... a great place to start.'
(A. M. Boughey)

'One of the best courses around to get you that little bit further than the basics.'
(Johannsen Krister)

more...

'The words are very clearly spoken and the form of presentation witty and lively to keep your interest, and clever choice of subject matter also keep learning interesting and aid memory. This is a very strong language course and I recommend it.'
(vh1967)

'The Elisabeth Smith courses are a superb resource for the learner who needs to be able to speak the language in a short period of time and with a good degree of understanding.'
(Will Boyce)

'I was surprised at what I'd achieved after this course and recommend it.'

'This is an absolute must have ... You'll be so glad you bought it!'
(Elodie)

Now join me on:

f Facebook at www.facebook.com/elisabethsmithlanguages

t Twitter at www.twitter.com/LanguagesESmith